GO!

with Microsoft®

Windows 7

Getting Started

Shelley Gaskin and Robert L. Ferrett

Prentice Hall

Boston Columbus Indianapolis New York San Francisco Upper Saddle River
Amsterdam Cape Town Dubai London Madrid Milan Munich Paris Montreal Toronto
Delhi Mexico City Sao Paulo Sydney Hong Kong Seoul Singapore Taipei Tokyo

Editor in Chief: Michael Payne
Associate VP/Executive Acquisitions Editor, Print: Stephanie Wall
Product Development Manager: Eileen Bien Calabro
Editorial Project Manager: Laura Burgess
Development Editor: Ginny Munroe
Editorial Assistant: Nicole Sam
Director of Marketing: Kate Valentine
Marketing Manager: Tori Olson Alves
Marketing Coordinator: Susan Osterlitz
Marketing Assistant: Darshika Vyas
Senior Managing Editor: Cynthia Zonneveld
Associate Managing Editor: Camille Trentacoste
Production Project Manager: Mike Lackey
Operations Director: Alexis Heydt
Operations Specialist: Natacha Moore
Senior Art Director: Jonathan Boylan
Text and Cover Designer: Blair Brown
Cover Photo: © Ben Durrant

Manager, Visual Research: Beth Brenzel
Manager, Rights and Permissions: Zina Arabia
Image Permission Coordinator: Richard Rodrigues
Manager, Cover Visual Research & Permissions: Karen Sanatar
Rights and Permissions Manager: Shannon Barbe
AVP/Director of Online Programs, Media: Richard Keaveny
AVP/Director of Product Development, Media: Lisa Strite
Product Development Manager, Media: Cathi Profitko
Media Project Manager, Editorial: Alana Coles
Media Project Manager, Production: John Cassar
Full-Service Project Management: GGS Higher Education Resources, a Division of Premedia Global, Inc.
Composition: GGS Higher Education Resources, a Division of Premedia Global, Inc.
Printer/Binder: Courier/Kendallville
Cover Printer: Lehigh-Phoenix Color/Hagerstown
Text Font: Bookman Light

Credits and acknowledgments borrowed from other sources and reproduced, with permission, in this textbook appear on appropriate page within text.

Microsoft® and Windows® are registered trademarks of the Microsoft Corporation in the U.S.A. and other countries. Screen shots and icons reprinted with permission from the Microsoft Corporation. This book is not sponsored or endorsed by or affiliated with the Microsoft Corporation.

Many of the designations by manufacturers and seller to distinguish their products are claimed as trademarks. Where those designations appear in this book, and the publisher was aware of a trademark claim, the designations have been printed in initial caps or all caps.

Library of Congress Cataloging-in-Publication Data

Gaskin, Shelley.
 Go! with Microsoft Windows 7. Getting started / by Shelley Gaskin and Robert L. Ferrett.
  p. cm.
 ISBN-13: 978-0-13-508831-9
 ISBN-10: 0-13-508831-3
 1. Microsoft Windows (Computer file) 2. Operating systems (Computers) I. Ferrett, Robert. II. Title.
 QA76.76.O63.G3924 2010
 005.4'46—dc22

                                                        2009048789

10 9 8 7 6

Prentice Hall
is an imprint of

www.pearsonhighered.com

ISBN-10: 0-13-508831-3
ISBN-13: 978-0-13-508831-9

Contents

GO! **Instructor Resources** .... **xii**

Windows 7

Chapter 1   Getting Started with Windows 1

PROJECT 1A   Familiarize Yourself with Windows 7 2

Objective 1   Get Started with Windows 7   **3**
Activity 1.1   Exploring the Windows 7 Desktop   3
Activity 1.2   Personalizing the Desktop   8
Activity 1.3   Adding and Removing Gadgets   11

Objective 2   Use the Start Menu and Manage Windows   **13**
Activity 1.4   Using the Start Menu   14
Activity 1.5   Adding Shortcuts to the Start Menu, Desktop, and Taskbar   16
Activity 1.6   Minimizing, Maximizing, and Restoring a Window   19
Activity 1.7   Hiding and Displaying Windows   20

Objective 3   Resize, Move, and Scroll Windows   **21**
Activity 1.8   Customizing and Using the Taskbar   22
Activity 1.9   Resizing, Moving, Scrolling, and Closing Windows   24

PROJECT 1B   Manage Files and Folders 28

Objective 4   Create, Move, and Rename Folders   **29**
Activity 1.10   Opening and Navigating Windows Explorer   29
Activity 1.11   Creating a New Folder   31
Activity 1.12   Moving and Renaming Folders   33

Objective 5   Copy, Move, Rename, and Delete Files   **35**
Activity 1.13   Copying Files   35
Activity 1.14   Moving, Renaming, and Deleting Files   37
Activity 1.15   Compressing Files   40
Activity 1.16   Using the Address Bar to Navigate Drives and Folders   42

Objective 6   Find Files and Folders   **43**
Activity 1.17   Adding Descriptions and Tags to Files   43
Activity 1.18   Finding Files and Folders and Creating a Search Folder   45
Summary   48
Key Terms   48
Screen ID   49
Matching   50
Multiple Choice   51
Skills Review   52

Glossary G-1

Index I-1

GO! System Contributors

We thank the following people for their hard work and support in making the GO! System all that it is!

Instructor Resource Authors

Paul Weaver	Bossier Parish Community College
Joyce Thompson	Lehigh Carbon Community College
Steve St. John	Tulsa Community College

Technical Editors

Jan Snyder
Janet Pickard

Student Reviewers

Albinda, Sarah Evangeline	Phoenix College	Innis, Tim	Tulsa Community College
Allen, John	Asheville-Buncombe Tech Community College	Jarboe, Aaron	Central Washington University
		Key, Penny	Greenville Technical College
Alexander, Steven	St. Johns River Community College	Klein, Colleen	Northern Michigan University
Alexander, Melissa	Tulsa Community College	Lloyd, Kasey	Ivy Tech Bloomington
Bolz, Stephanie	Northern Michigan University	Moeller, Jeffrey	Northern Michigan University
Berner, Ashley	Central Washington University	Mullen, Sharita	Tidewater Community College
Boomer, Michelle	Northern Michigan University	Nelson, Cody	Texas Tech University
Busse, Brennan	Northern Michigan University	Nicholson, Regina	Athens Tech College
Butkey, Maura	Central Washington University	Niehaus, Kristina	Northern Michigan University
Cates, Concita	Phoenix College	Nisa, Zaibun	Santa Rosa Community College
Charles, Marvin	Harrisburg Area Community College	Nunez, Nohelia	Santa Rosa Community College
		Oak, Samantha	Central Washington University
Christensen, Kaylie	Northern Michigan University	Oberly, Sara	Harrisburg Area Community College Lancaster
Clark, Glen D. III	Harrisburg Area Community College		
		Oertii, Monica	Central Washington University
Cobble, Jan N.	Greenville Technical College	Palenshus, Juliet	Central Washington University
Connally, Brianna	Central Washington University	Pohl, Amanda	Northern Michigan University
Davis, Brandon	Northern Michigan University	Presnell, Randy	Central Washington University
Davis, Christen	Central Washington University	Reed, Kailee	Texas Tech University
De Jesus Garcia, Maria	Phoenix College	Ritner, April	Northern Michigan University
Den Boer, Lance	Central Washington University	Roberts, Corey	Tulsa Community College
Dix, Jessica	Central Washington University	Rodgers, Spencer	Texas Tech University
Moeller, Jeffrey	Northern Michigan University	Rodriguez, Flavia	Northwestern State University
Downs, Elizabeth	Central Washington University	Rogers, A.	Tidewater Community College
Elser, Julie	Harrisburg Area Community College	Rossi, Jessica Ann	Central Washington University
		Rothbauer, Taylor	Trident Technical College
Erickson, Mike	Ball State University	Rozelle, Lauren	Texas Tech University
Frye, Alicia	Phoenix College	Schmadeke, Kimberly	Kirkwood Community College
Gadomski, Amanda	Northern Michigan University	Shafapay, Natasha	Central Washington University
Gassert, Jennifer	Harrisburg Area Community College	Shanahan, Megan	Northern Michigan University
		Sullivan, Alexandra Nicole	Greenville Technical College
Gross, Mary Jo	Kirkwood Community College	Teska, Erika	Hawaii Pacific University
Gyselinck, Craig	Central Washington University	Torrenti, Natalie	Harrisburg Area Community College
Harrison, Margo	Central Washington University		
Hatt, Patrick	Harrisburg Area Community College	Traub, Amy	Northern Michigan University
Heacox, Kate	Central Washington University	Underwood, Katie	Central Washington University
Hedgman, Shaina	Tidewater College	Walters, Kim	Central Washington University
Hill, Cheretta	Northwestern State University	Warren, Jennifer L.	Greenville Technical College
Hochstedler, Bethany	Harrisburg Area Community College Lancaster	Wilson, Kelsie	Central Washington University
		Wilson, Amanda	Green River Community College
Homer, Jean	Greenville Technical College	Wylie, Jimmy	Texas Tech University

Contributors continued

Ecklund, Paula	Duke University	Hotta, Barbara	Leeward Community College
Eilers, Albert	Cincinnati State Technical and Community College	Howard, Bunny	St. Johns River Community
		Howard, Chris	DeVry University
Eng, Bernice	Brookdale Community College	Huckabay, Jamie	Austin Community College
Epperson, Arlin	Columbia College	Hudgins, Susan	East Central University
Evans, Billie	Vance-Granville Community College	Hulett, Michelle J.	Missouri State University
		Humphrey, John	Asheville Buncombe Technical Community College
Evans, Jean	Brevard Community College		
Feuerbach, Lisa	Ivy Tech East Chicago	Hunt, Darla A.	Morehead State University, Morehead, Kentucky
Finley, Jean	ABTCC		
Fisher, Fred	Florida State University	Hunt, Laura	Tulsa Community College
Foster, Nancy	Baker College	Ivey, Joan M.	Lanier Technical College
Foster-Shriver, Penny L.	Anne Arundel Community College	Jacob, Sherry	Jefferson Community College
		Jacobs, Duane	Salt Lake Community College
Foster-Turpen, Linda	CNM	Jauken, Barb	Southeastern Community
Foszcz, Russ	McHenry County College	Jerry, Gina	Santa Monica College
Fry, Susan	Boise State University	Johnson, Deborah S.	Edison State College
Fustos, Janos	Metro State	Johnson, Kathy	Wright College
Gallup, Jeanette	Blinn College	Johnson, Mary	Kingwood College
Gelb, Janet	Grossmont College	Johnson, Mary	Mt. San Antonio College
Gentry, Barb	Parkland College	Jones, Stacey	Benedict College
Gerace, Karin	St. Angela Merici School	Jones, Warren	University of Alabama, Birmingham
Gerace, Tom	Tulane University		
Ghajar, Homa	Oklahoma State University	Jordan, Cheryl	San Juan College
Gifford, Steve	Northwest Iowa Community College	Kapoor, Bhushan	California State University, Fullerton
Glazer, Ellen	Broward Community College	Kasai, Susumu	Salt Lake Community College
Gordon, Robert	Hofstra University	Kates, Hazel	Miami Dade Community College, Kendall
Gramlich, Steven	Pasco-Hernando Community College		
		Keen, Debby	University of Kentucky
Graviett, Nancy M.	St. Charles Community College, St. Peters, Missouri	Keeter, Sandy	Seminole Community College
		Kern-Blystone, Dorothy Jean	Bowling Green State
Greene, Rich	Community College of Allegheny County	Kerwin, Annette	College of DuPage
		Keskin, Ilknur	The University of South Dakota
Gregoryk, Kerry	Virginia Commonwealth State	Kinney, Mark B.	Baker College
Griggs, Debra	Bellevue Community College	Kirk, Colleen	Mercy College
Grimm, Carol	Palm Beach Community College	Kisling, Eric	East Carolina University
Guthrie, Rose	Fox Valley Technical College	Kleckner, Michelle	Elon University
Hahn, Norm	Thomas Nelson Community College	Kliston, Linda	Broward Community College, North Campus
Haley-Hunter, Deb	Bluefield State College	Knuth, Toni	Baker College of Auburn Hills
Hall, Linnea	Northwest Mississippi Community College	Kochis, Dennis	Suffolk County Community College
Hammerschlag, Dr. Bill	Brookhaven College	Kominek, Kurt	Northeast State Technical Community College
Hansen, Michelle	Davenport University		
Hayden, Nancy	Indiana University—Purdue University, Indianapolis	Kramer, Ed	Northern Virginia Community College
		Kretz, Daniel	Fox Valley Technical College
Hayes, Theresa	Broward Community College	Laird, Jeff	Northeast State Community College
Headrick, Betsy	Chattanooga State		
Helfand, Terri	Chaffey College	Lamoureaux, Jackie	Central New Mexico Community College
Helms, Liz	Columbus State Community College		
		Lange, David	Grand Valley State
Hernandez, Leticia	TCI College of Technology	LaPointe, Deb	Central New Mexico Community College
Hibbert, Marilyn	Salt Lake Community College		
Hinds, Cheryl	Norfolk State University	Larsen, Jacqueline Anne	A-B Tech
Hines, James	Tidewater Community College	Larson, Donna	Louisville Technical Institute
Hoffman, Joan	Milwaukee Area Technical College	Laspina, Kathy	Vance-Granville Community College
Hogan, Pat	Cape Fear Community College	Le Grand, Dr. Kate	Broward Community College
Holland, Susan	Southeast Community College	Lenhart, Sheryl	Terra Community College
Holliday, Mardi	Community College of Philadelphia	Leonard, Yvonne	Coastal Carolina Community College
Hollingsworth, Mary Carole	Georgia Perimeter College		
		Letavec, Chris	University of Cincinnati
Hopson, Bonnie	Athens Technical College	Lewis, Daphne L., Ed.D.	Wayland Baptist University
Horvath, Carrie	Albertus Magnus College	Lewis, Julie	Baker College-Allen Park
Horwitz, Steve	Community College of Philadelphia	Liefert, Jane	Everett Community College

Lindaman, Linda	Black Hawk Community College	Meredith, Mary	University of Louisiana at Lafayette
Lindberg, Martha	Minnesota State University	Mermelstein, Lisa	Baruch College
Lightner, Renee	Broward Community College	Metos, Linda	Salt Lake Community College
Lindberg, Martha	Minnesota State University	Meurer, Daniel	University of Cincinnati
Linge, Richard	Arizona Western College	Meyer, Colleen	Cincinnati State Technical and Community College
Logan, Mary G.	Delgado Community College		
Loizeaux, Barbara	Westchester Community College	Meyer, Marian	Central New Mexico Community College
Lombardi, John	South University		
Lopez, Don	Clovis-State Center Community College District	Miller, Cindy	Ivy Tech Community College, Lafayette, Indiana
Lopez, Lisa	Spartanburg Community College	Mills, Robert E.	Tidewater Community College, Portsmouth Campus
Lord, Alexandria	Asheville Buncombe Tech		
Lovering, LeAnne	Augusta Technical College	Mitchell, Susan	Davenport University
Lowe, Rita	Harold Washington College	Mohle, Dennis	Fresno Community College
Low, Willy Hui	Joliet Junior College	Molki, Saeed	South Texas College
Lucas, Vickie	Broward Community College	Monk, Ellen	University of Delaware
Luna, Debbie	El Paso Community College	Moore, Rodney	Holland College
Luoma, Jean	Davenport University	Morris, Mike	Southeastern Oklahoma State University
Luse, Steven P.	Horry Georgetown Technical College		
Lynam, Linda	Central Missouri State University	Morris, Nancy	Hudson Valley Community College
Lyon, Lynne	Durham College	Moseler, Dan	Harrisburg Area Community College
Lyon, Pat Rajski	Tomball College		
Macarty, Matthew	University of New Hampshire	Nabors, Brent	Reedley College, Clovis Center
MacKinnon, Ruth	Georgia Southern University	Nadas, Erika	Wright College
Macon, Lisa	Valencia Community College, West Campus	Nadelman, Cindi	New England College
		Nademlynsky, Lisa	Johnson & Wales University
Machuca, Wayne	College of the Sequoias	Nagengast, Joseph	Florida Career College
Mack, Sherri	Butler County Community College	Nason, Scott	Rowan Cabarrus Community College
Madison, Dana	Clarion University		
Maguire, Trish	Eastern New Mexico University	Ncube, Cathy	University of West Florida
Malkan, Rajiv	Montgomery College	Newsome, Eloise	Northern Virginia Community College Woodbridge
Manning, David	Northern Kentucky University		
Marcus, Jacquie	Niagara Community College	Nicholls, Doreen	Mohawk Valley Community College
Marghitu, Daniela	Auburn University		
Marks, Suzanne	Bellevue Community College	Nicholson, John R.	Johnson County Community College
Marquez, Juanita	El Centro College		
Marquez, Juan	Mesa Community College	Nielson, Phil	Salt Lake Community College
Martin, Carol	Harrisburg Area Community College	Nunan, Karen L.	Northeast State Technical Community College
Martin, Paul C.	Harrisburg Area Community College	O'Neal, Lois Ann	Rogers State University
		Odegard, Teri	Edmonds Community College
Martyn, Margie	Baldwin-Wallace College	Ogle, Gregory	North Community College
Marucco, Toni	Lincoln Land Community College	Orr, Dr. Claudia	Northern Michigan University South
Mason, Lynn	Lubbock Christian University		
Matutis, Audrone	Houston Community College	Orsburn, Glen	Fox Valley Technical College
Matkin, Marie	University of Lethbridge	Otieno, Derek	DeVry University
Maurel, Trina	Odessa College	Otton, Diana Hill	Chesapeake College
May, Karen	Blinn College	Oxendale, Lucia	West Virginia Institute of Technology
McCain, Evelynn	Boise State University		
McCannon, Melinda	Gordon College	Paiano, Frank	Southwestern College
McCarthy, Marguerite	Northwestern Business College	Pannell, Dr. Elizabeth	Collin College
McCaskill, Matt L.	Brevard Community College	Patrick, Tanya	Clackamas Community College
McClellan, Carolyn	Tidewater Community College	Paul, Anindya	Daytona State College
McClure, Darlean	College of Sequoias	Peairs, Deb	Clark State Community College
McCrory, Sue A.	Missouri State University	Perez, Kimberly	Tidewater Community College
McCue, Stacy	Harrisburg Area Community College	Porter, Joyce	Weber State University
		Prince, Lisa	Missouri State University-Springfield Campus
McEntire-Orbach, Teresa	Middlesex County College		
McKinley, Lee	Georgia Perimeter College	Proietti, Kathleen	Northern Essex Community College
McLeod, Todd	Fresno City College		
McManus, Illyana	Grossmont College	Puopolo, Mike	Bunker Hill Community College
McPherson, Dori	Schoolcraft College	Pusins, Delores	HCCC
Meck, Kari	HACC	Putnam, Darlene	Thomas Nelson Community College
Meiklejohn, Nancy	Pikes Peak Community College		
Menking, Rick	Hardin-Simmons University		

Raghuraman, Ram — Joliet Junior College
Rani, Chigurupati — BMCC/CUNY
Reasoner, Ted Allen — Indiana University—Purdue
Reeves, Karen — High Point University
Remillard, Debbie — New Hampshire Technical Institute
Rhue, Shelly — DeVry University
Richards, Karen — Maplewoods Community College
Richardson, Mary — Albany Technical College
Rodgers, Gwen — Southern Nazarene University
Rodie, Karla — Pikes Peak Community College
Roselli, Diane Maie — Harrisburg Area Community College
Ross, Dianne — University of Louisiana in Lafayette
Rousseau, Mary — Broward Community College, South
Rovetto, Ann — Horry-Georgetown Technical College
Rusin, Iwona — Baker College
Sahabi, Ahmad — Baker College of Clinton Township
Samson, Dolly — Hawaii Pacific University
Sams, Todd — University of Cincinnati
Sandoval, Everett — Reedley College
Santiago, Diana — Central New Mexico Community College
Sardone, Nancy — Seton Hall University
Scafide, Jean — Mississippi Gulf Coast Community College
Scheeren, Judy — Westmoreland County Community College
Scheiwe, Adolph — Joliet Junior College
Schneider, Sol — Sam Houston State University
Schweitzer, John — Central New Mexico Community College
Scroggins, Michael — Southwest Missouri State University
Sedlacek, Brenda — Tidewater Community College
Sell, Kelly — Anne Arundel Community College
Sever, Suzanne — Northwest Arkansas Community College
Sewell, John — Florida Career College
Sheridan, Rick — California State University-Chico
Silvers, Pamela — Asheville Buncombe Tech
Sindt, Robert G. — Johnson County Community College
Singer, Noah — Tulsa Community College
Singer, Steven A. — University of Hawai'i, Kapi'olani Community College
Sinha, Atin — Albany State University
Skolnick, Martin — Florida Atlantic University
Smith, Kristi — Allegany College of Maryland
Smith, Patrick — Marshall Community and Technical College
Smith, Stella A. — Georgia Gwinnett College
Smith, T. Michael — Austin Community College
Smith, Tammy — Tompkins Cortland Community Collge
Smolenski, Bob — Delaware County Community College
Smolenski, Robert — Delaware Community College
Southwell, Donald — Delta College
Spangler, Candice — Columbus State
Spangler, Candice — Columbus State Community College
Stark, Diane — Phoenix College
Stedham, Vicki — St. Petersburg College, Clearwater
Stefanelli, Greg — Carroll Community College
Steiner, Ester — New Mexico State University
Stenlund, Neal — Northern Virginia Community College, Alexandria
St. John, Steve — Tulsa Community College
Sterling, Janet — Houston Community College
Stoughton, Catherine — Laramie County Community College
Sullivan, Angela — Joliet Junior College

Sullivan, Denise — Westchester Community College
Sullivan, Joseph — Joliet Junior College
Swart, John — Louisiana Tech University
Szurek, Joseph — University of Pittsburgh at Greensburg
Taff, Ann — Tulsa Community College
Taggart, James — Atlantic Cape Community College
Tarver, Mary Beth — Northwestern State University
Taylor, Michael — Seattle Central Community College
Terrell, Robert L. — Carson-Newman College
Terry, Dariel — Northern Virginia Community College
Thangiah, Sam — Slippery Rock University
Thayer, Paul — Austin Community College
Thompson, Joyce — Lehigh Carbon Community College
Thompson-Sellers, Ingrid — Georgia Perimeter College
Tomasi, Erik — Baruch College
Toreson, Karen — Shoreline Community College
Townsend, Cynthia — Baker College
Trifiletti, John J. — Florida Community College at Jacksonville
Trivedi, Charulata — Quinsigamond Community College, Woodbridge
Tucker, William — Austin Community College
Turgeon, Cheryl — Asnuntuck Community College
Turpen, Linda — Central New Mexico Community College
Upshaw, Susan — Del Mar College
Unruh, Angela — Central Washington University
Vanderhoof, Dr. Glenna — Missouri State University-Springfield Campus
Vargas, Tony — El Paso Community College
Vicars, Mitzi — Hampton University
Villarreal, Kathleen — Fresno
Vitrano, Mary Ellen — Palm Beach Community College
Vlaich-Lee, Michelle — Greenville Technical College
Volker, Bonita — Tidewater Community College
Waddell, Karen — Butler Community College
Wahila, Lori (Mindy) — Tompkins Cortland Community College
Wallace, Melissa — Lanier Technical College
Walters, Gary B. — Central New Mexico Community College
Waswick, Kim — Southeast Community College, Nebraska
Wavle, Sharon M. — Tompkins Cortland Community College
Webb, Nancy — City College of San Francisco
Webb, Rebecca — Northwest Arkansas Community College
Weber, Sandy — Gateway Technical College
Weissman, Jonathan — Finger Lakes Community College
Wells, Barbara E. — Central Carolina Technical College
Wells, Lorna — Salt Lake Community College
Welsh, Jean — Lansing Community College Nebraska
White, Bruce — Quinnipiac University
Willer, Ann — Solano Community College
Williams, Mark — Lane Community College
Williams, Ronald D. — Central Piedmont Community College
Wilms, Dr. G. Jan — Union University
Wilson, Kit — Red River College
Wilson, MaryLou — Piedmont Technical College
Wilson, Roger — Fairmont State University
Wimberly, Leanne — International Academy of Design and Technology

Winters, Floyd	Manatee Community College	Yip, Thomas	Passaic Community College
Worthington, Paula	Northern Virginia Community College	Zavala, Ben	Webster Tech
		Zaboski, Maureen	University of Scranton
Wright, Darrell	Shelton State Community College	Zlotow, Mary Ann	College of DuPage
Wright, Julie	Baker College	Zudeck, Steve	Broward Community College, North
Yauney, Annette	Herkimer County Community College	Zullo, Matthew D.	Wake Technical Community College

About the Authors

Shelley Gaskin, Series Editor, is a professor of business and computer technology at Pasadena City College in Pasadena, California. She holds a master's degree in business education from Northern Illinois University and a doctorate in adult and community education from Ball State University. Dr. Gaskin has 15 years of experience in the computer industry with several Fortune 500 companies and has developed and written training materials for custom systems applications in both the public and private sector. She is also the author of books on Microsoft Outlook and word processing.

Robert L. Ferrett recently retired as the director of the Center for Instructional Computing at Eastern Michigan University, where he provided computer training and support to faculty. He has authored or co-authored more than 70 books on Access, PowerPoint, Excel, Publisher, WordPerfect, and Word. Before writing for the GO! Series, Bob was a series editor and author for the Learn Series. He has a bachelor's degree in psychology, a master's degree in geography, and a master's degree in interdisciplinary technology from Eastern Michigan University. Bob's doctoral studies were in instructional technology at Wayne State University. For fun, Bob teaches a four-week computers and genealogy class and has written genealogy and local history books.

GO! Instructor Materials

The following instructor materials are available on either the instructors resource CD or www.pearsonhighered.com/go

Annotated Solution Files
Coupled with the assignment tags this creates a grading and scoring system that makes grading so much easier for you

Assignment Sheets
Lists all the assignments for the chapter, you just add in the course information, due dates and points. Providing these to students ensures they will know what is due and when

Point-Counted Production Tests
Exams for each project and chapter

Power Point Lectures
PowerPoint presentations for each chapter

Scorecards
Can be used either by students to check their work or by you as a quick check-off for the items that need to be corrected

Solution Files
Answers to the projects in the book

Scripted Lectures
Classroom lectures prepared for you

Test Bank
Includes a variety of test questions for each chapter

Companion Web Site
Online content such as the Online Study Guide, Glossary, and Student Data Files are all at www.pearsonhighered.com/go

Getting Started with Windows 7

OUTCOMES

At the end of this chapter, you will be able to:

OBJECTIVES

Mastering these objectives will enable you to:

PROJECT 1A
Familiarize Yourself
with Windows 7.

1. Get Started with Windows 7 (p. 3)
2. Use the Start Menu and Manage Windows (p. 13)
3. Resize, Move, and Scroll Windows (p. 21)

PROJECT 1B
Manage Files and Folders.

4. Create, Move, and Rename Folders (p. 29)
5. Copy, Move, Rename, and Delete Files (p. 35)
6. Find Files and Folders (p. 43)

Dmitriy Shironosov/Shutterstock

In This Chapter

Windows 7 is the software that coordinates the activities of your computer's hardware. Windows 7 controls how your screen is displayed, how you open and close programs, and the start-up, shut-down, and navigation procedures for your computer. It is useful to become familiar with the basic features of the Microsoft Windows operating system, especially working with the Start button and the taskbar; opening, closing, moving, and resizing windows; and finding, saving, and managing files and folders.

Project 1A Familiarize Yourself with Windows 7

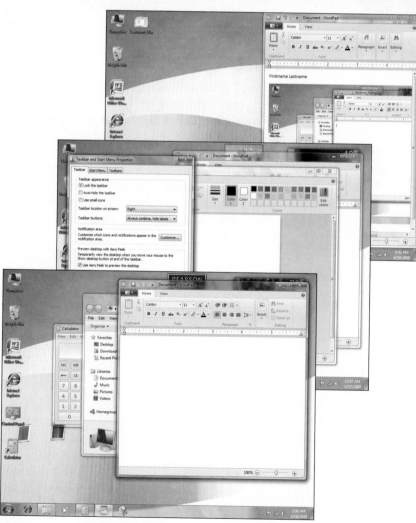

Figure 1.1

Objective 1 | Get Started with Windows 7

Windows 7 is an *operating system*—software that controls the *hardware* attached to your computer, including its memory, disk drive space, attached devices such as printers and scanners, and the central processing unit. Windows 7 and earlier versions of Windows are similar; they use a *graphical user interface (GUI)*. A GUI uses graphics or pictures to represent commands and actions and lets you see document formatting on the screen as it will look when printed on paper. *Windows*, when spelled with a capital *W*, refers to the operating system that runs your computer.

Starting Windows is an automatic procedure; you turn on your computer, and after a few moments, the version of Windows installed on your computer displays. Some computers require that you log in, and some do not. Windows 7 is available in several versions: Starter, Home Premium, Professional, and Ultimate. For large institutions, there is also an Enterprise edition. For most tasks, the Home Premium, Professional, and Ultimate editions work the same. The Starter edition is typically used only on small notebook computers.

Alert! | Does your screen differ?

This chapter uses Windows 7 Ultimate edition, and there may be some differences in the look of this edition and the other editions. More importantly, the look of the screen will depend largely on the setting options that have been selected for your computer, the shape of your monitor, and on the type of hardware installed in your computer—especially the video card and memory.

Activity 1.01 | Exploring the Windows 7 Desktop

In this activity, you will examine the different components of the Windows 7 desktop.

1 Turn on your computer and wait for the Windows program to display, or follow the log-on instructions required for the computer you are using. For example, you might have to click a name on a Welcome screen, or enter a user ID or password. If this is your home computer and you are the only user, it is likely that you need do nothing except wait for a few moments.

The Windows *desktop*, which is the working area of the Windows 7 screen, displays. The screen look will vary, depending on which version of Windows you are using and what you have on your own desktop.

2 Compare your Windows desktop with Figure 1.2 and then take a moment to study the Windows elements identified in the table in Figure 1.3. Your icons may vary.

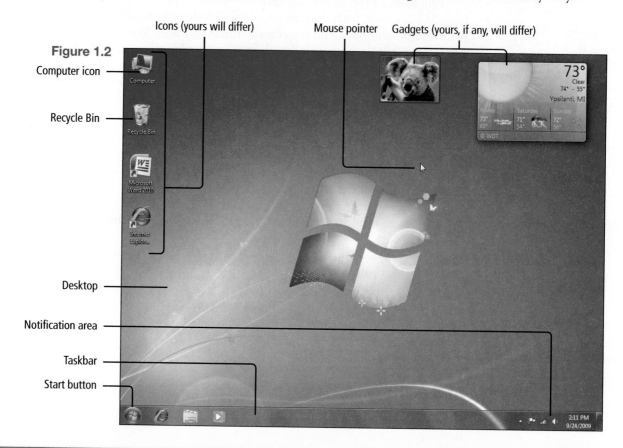

Figure 1.2

Windows Screen Elements

Screen Element	Description
Command bar	A toolbar that offers easy access to settings or features.
Computer icon	An icon that represents the computer on which you are working, and that provides access to the drives, folders, and files on your computer.
Desktop	The working area of the Windows 7 screen, consisting of program icons, a taskbar, gadgets (optional), and a Start button.
Gadgets	Small dynamic programs that run on the desktop, such as a clock, a stock market ticker, or a weather forecast.
Icon	A graphic representation of an object that you can select and open, such as a drive, a disk, a folder, a document, or a program.
Mouse pointer	The arrow, I-beam, or other symbol that moves when you move the mouse or other pointing device, and that indicates a location or position on your screen—also called the *pointer*.
Notification area	The area on the right side of the taskbar, formerly called the *system tray* or *status area*, where the clock and system notifications display. These notifications keep you informed about active processes.
Recycle Bin	A temporary storage area for files that you have deleted from hard drives. Files can be either recovered or permanently removed from the Recycle Bin.
Start button	The button on the left side of the taskbar that is used to start programs, change system settings, find Windows help, search for programs or documents, or shut down the computer.
Taskbar	Displays the Start button and icons for any open programs. The taskbar also displays shortcut buttons for other programs.

Figure 1.3

3 On the left side of the taskbar, *click*—press the left mouse button one time—the **Windows Explorer** button 📁. Compare your screen with Figure 1.4, and then take a moment to study the *Windows Explorer* window elements in the table in Figure 1.5. **Windows Explorer** is a program used to create and manage folders, and to copy, move, sort, and delete files. If the Windows Explorer button does not display on your taskbar, click the Start button, click All Programs, click Accessories, and then click Windows Explorer. If the Menu bar does not display, on the Toolbar, click the Organize button, point to Layout, and then click Menu bar.

The Windows Explorer window displays. When you click the Windows Explorer button, the window opens with *Libraries* selected in the Navigation pane and displayed in the file list. A *window*—spelled with a lowercase *w*—is a rectangular box that displays information or a program. When a window is open, the name of the window is sometimes displayed in the title bar.

Alert! | Does your screen differ?

Because the configuration of your Windows Explorer window depends on how it was last used, your window may not display all of the elements shown in Figure 1.4, in particular the Menu bar, Details pane, Navigation pane, and Search pane. A Preview pane may display on the right side of the window, and the window may cover the entire screen.

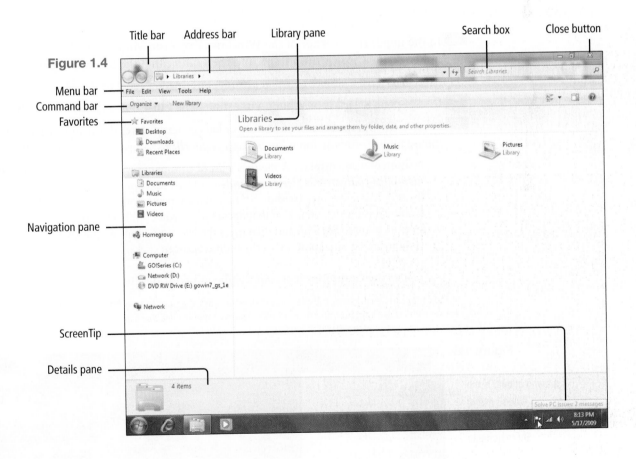

Figure 1.4

Title bar   Address bar   Library pane   Search box   Close button

Menu bar
Command bar
Favorites
Navigation pane
ScreenTip
Details pane

Parts of a Window

Screen Element	Description
Address bar	A toolbar that displays the organizational path to the active file, folder, or window.
Close button	A button in a title bar that closes a window or a Program
Details pane	Displays details about the drive, folder, or file selected in the file list.
Favorites	The upper part of the Navigation pane that displays favorite destinations associated with the current user.
File list	Displays the contents of the current folder or library.
Library pane	Displays above the file list when a Library is selected in the Navigation pane.
Menu bar	The bar near the top of a window that lists the names of menu categories.
Navigation pane	The pane on the left side of the Windows Explorer window that contains personal Favorites, Libraries, access to personal files and folders, and other items.
ScreenTip	A small box, activated by pointing to a button or other screen object, that displays the name of or further information about the screen element.
Search box	A box in which you type a search word or phrase.
Title bar	The area at the top of a window that includes the Minimize, Maximize, and Close buttons. The title bar also often contains the name of the program and the name of the open document.
Toolbar	A row of buttons that activates commands with a single click of the left mouse button.

Figure 1.5

4 In the upper right corner of the **Windows Explorer** window title bar, point to, but do not click, the **Close** button ⊠, and then notice that the ScreenTip *Close* displays.

> A *ScreenTip* is a small note that provides information about or describes a screen element.

5 Click—press the left mouse button one time—the **Close** button ⊠ to close the window.

6 Point to the **Computer** icon in the upper left corner of the desktop and click the right mouse button—this action is known as a *right-click*. Compare your screen with Figure 1.6.

> A shortcut menu displays. A *menu* is a list of commands within a category. *Shortcut menus* list *context-sensitive commands*—commands commonly used when working with the selected object. On this shortcut menu, the Open command is displayed in bold because it is the default action that occurs when you double-click this icon. To *double-click* an icon, point to the icon and then press the left mouse button quickly two times in succession, taking care not to move the mouse between clicks.

Alert! | Does the Computer icon not display on your desktop?

If the Computer icon does not display on the desktop, click the Start button 🌐. On the right side of the Start menu, right-click Computer, and then from the shortcut menu, click *Show on Desktop*.

Figure 1.6

Command in bold is the default action

Shortcut menu

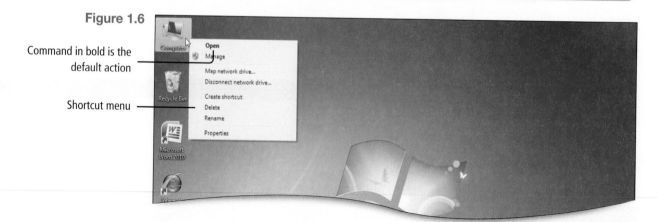

7 From the displayed shortcut menu, point to **Open** to select the command, and then click one time. Compare your screen with Figure 1.7.

> The Windows Explorer window displays, but this time the pane on the right is a file list, not a Libraries pane. The *file list* displays the contents of the item selected in the Navigation pane; in this case, the fixed and removable drives attached to the computer. A *drive* is an area of storage that is formatted with the Windows file system, and that has a drive letter such as C, D, E, and so on. The main drive inside your computer is referred to as the *hard drive*—there may be more than one hard drive in a computer. Also, network drives may display here.

Figure 1.7

Fixed local drives

Removable drives

File list

8 Near the top of the **file list**, point to and then click the disk drive labeled **(C:)**, and then notice the **Details** pane. Compare your screen with Figure 1.8.

Figure 1.8

Drive C: selected

Details of drive C: (your
drive name may vary)

> **Alert! | Is your Details pane missing?**
>
> Recall that the configuration of your Windows Explorer window may vary, depending on how it was last configured. If your Details pane does not display, in the Command bar, click Organize, point to Layout, and then click *Details pane*.

9 In the **Windows Explorer** window title bar, click the **Close** button ☒.

> **More Knowledge | The Windows Aero User Interface**
>
> The screen you see in the figures in this book uses the Windows Aero user interface. **Windows Aero**—which is an acronym for *A*uthentic, *E*nergetic, *R*eflective, *O*pen—features a three-dimensional look, with transparent window frames, live previews of open windows, and multiple color schemes. This user interface is available with all but the most basic versions of Windows 7, but requires extra memory and a good video card. If your screen does not have the same look, your computer may not be capable of displaying the Aero interface.

Activity 1.02 | Personalizing the Desktop

The Windows 7 desktop can be personalized to suit your needs and tastes. You can, for example, change the resolution of the monitor to make it easier to read or display more information. In this activity, you will change the icons displayed on the desktop, change the screen saver, and change the desktop background.

1 Move the pointer to an open area of the desktop, and then right-click.

A shortcut menu displays commands that are available for your desktop.

2 From the shortcut menu, move the pointer to the bottom of the list, and then click **Personalize**. Notice that the Personalization window displays, as shown in Figure 1.9.

Figure 1.9
Personalization window —
Desktop background options —
Current background picture —

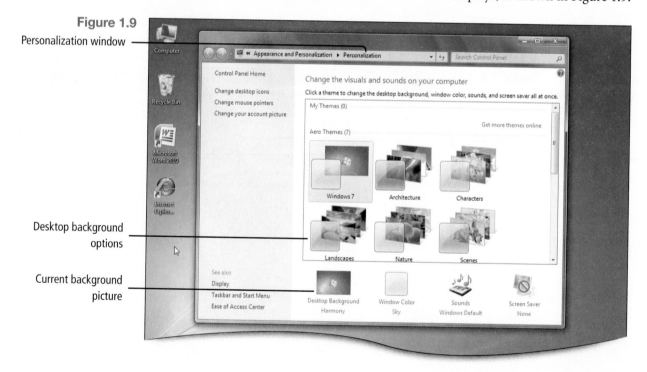

3 In the lower right corner of the **Personalization** window, click **Screen Saver**.

A *screen saver* is a picture or animation that displays on your screen after a preset period of computer inactivity.

4 In the **Screen Saver Settings** dialog box, click the **Screen saver box arrow**. From the displayed list, click **Ribbons**, and then compare your screen with Figure 1.10.

A *dialog box* is a box that asks you to make a decision about an individual object or topic. The Ribbons screen saver is selected, and a preview displays near the top of the dialog box. The default length of inactivity to trigger the screen saver is 1 minute.

Figure 1.10

Preview of Ribbons screen saver

Screen saver box arrow

Selected screen saver

Period of inactivity before screen saver displays

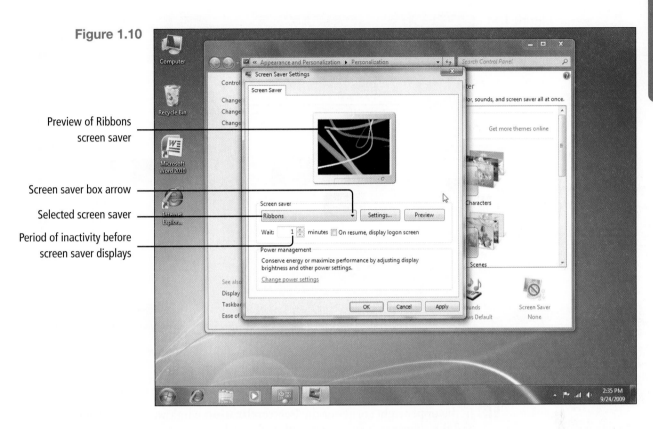

5 In the **Screen Saver Settings** dialog box, click the **Preview** button to preview a full-screen version of the screen saver. When you are through, move the mouse to turn off the full-screen screen saver preview. If you want to turn on the screen saver, click **OK**; otherwise, click **Cancel**.

6 In the left panel of the **Personalization** window, click **Change desktop icons**.

7 At the top of the **Desktop Icon Settings** dialog box, select—click to add a check mark to—the **Control Panel** check box. Click **OK** to save your changes and close the Desktop Icon Settings dialog box. Notice that a Control Panel icon is added to the left side of the desktop.

8 At the bottom of the **Personalization** window, click **Desktop Background**. Click the **up arrow** ▲ at the top of the scroll bar several times to move to the top of the backgrounds list. Under **Architecture**, click the third picture—the picture of the white building. The new background previews on the screen, as shown in Figure 1.11.

The *desktop background* is the picture, pattern, or color that displays on the desktop.

Figure 1.11

Selected background

Architecture backgrounds

Selected background previewed on the desktop

New desktop icon

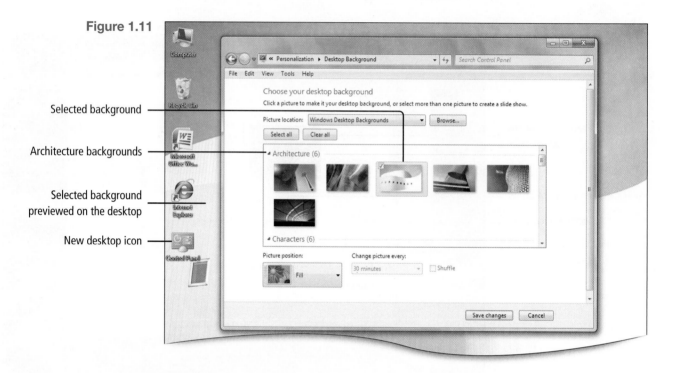

9 At the bottom of the **Personalization** window, click **Save changes**.

10 In the upper right corner of the **Personalization** window, click the **Close** button ⊠, and then compare your screen with Figure 1.12.

Figure 1.12

New background applied to desktop

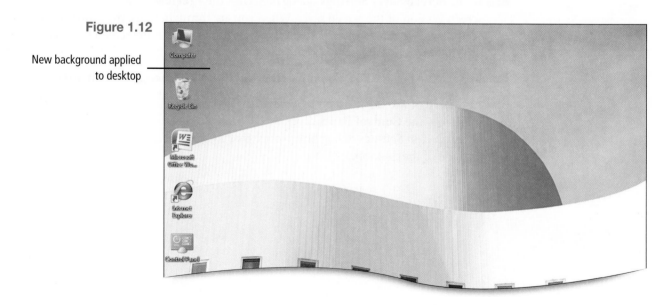

Activity 1.03 | Adding and Removing Gadgets

Gadgets are used to display dynamic programs such as a currency converter, a calendar, a stock market ticker, or a clock. You can move the gadgets anywhere on the screen, and you can modify or resize most of them.

1 In an open area of the desktop, right-click to display a shortcut menu. On the shortcut menu, click **Gadgets**. Compare your screen with Figure 1.13.

Figure 1.13

Gadgets available on your computer

Online link to other gadgets

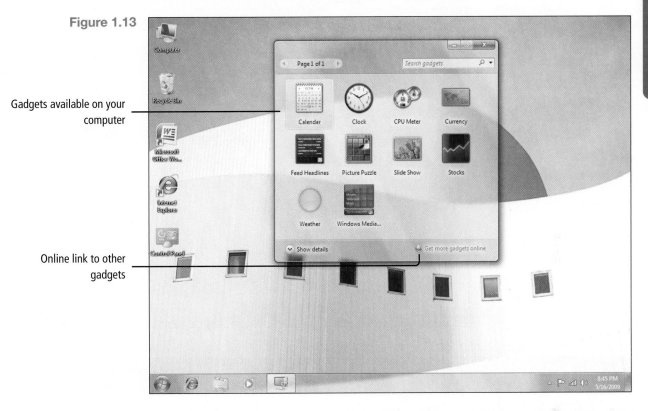

2 In the **Gadgets** window, double-click the **Weather** gadget. In the upper right corner of the **Gadgets** dialog box, click the **Close** button ▨.

Alert! | Are there already gadgets on your desktop?

Your desktop may contain one or more gadgets, including a Weather gadget. In fact, you can have more than one of the same gadgets on the desktop at a time. For example, if you are interested in the weather in two different locations, you can add two weather gadgets to the desktop and keep an eye on two locations at one time.

---

3 Point to the **Weather** gadget. Notice that a four-button tool set, called the *gadget controls*, displays on the right, as shown in Figure 1.14. Take a moment to study the functions of the buttons, as shown in the table in Figure 1.15.

Figure 1.14

Weather gadget

Gadget controls

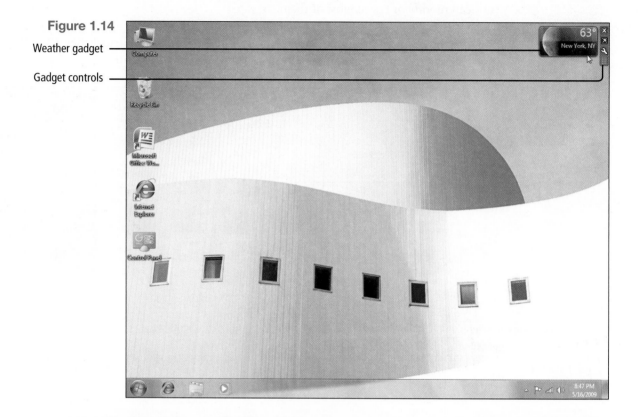

Gadget Controls

Button Name	Button	Description
Close	X	Closes the gadget.
Larger size	↗	Increases the size of the gadget; occupies the same position as the Smaller size button.
Smaller size	↰	Decreases the size of the gadget; occupies the same position as the Larger size button.
Options	🔧	Displays different settings for each gadget.
Drag gadget	⣿	Used to move the gadget anywhere on the desktop.

Figure 1.15

4 Point to the **Weather** gadget, click the **Larger size** button ⬈, and then click the **Options** button 🔍. In the **Select current location** box, type **Madison, Wisconsin** and then press [Enter]. Click **OK**, and then compare your screen with Figure 1.16.

Figure 1.16

Weather gadget enlarged —

Selected city —

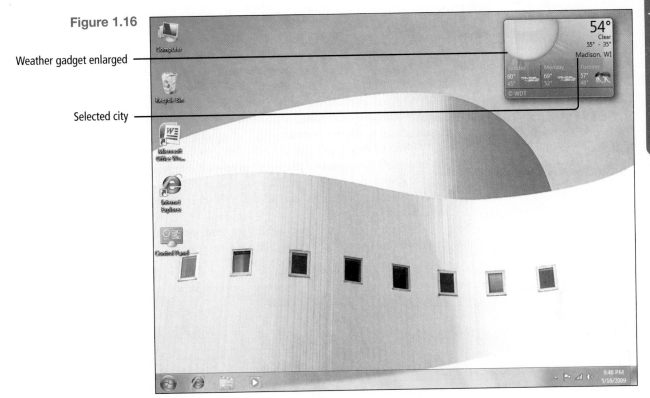

5 In an open area of the desktop, right-click to display a shortcut menu. On the short-cut menu, click **Gadgets**. In the **Gadgets** window, double-click the **Slide Show** gadget, and then double-click the **Slide Show** gadget again. In the upper right corner of the **Gadgets** dialog box, click the **Close** button 🅧.

Two additional gadgets are added to the desktop.

6 Point to either of the **Slide Show** gadgets, and then in the gadget controls, click the **Close** button 🅧 to remove the gadget from the desktop.

7 Point to the remaining **Slide Show** gadget, point to the **Drag gadget** button ⊞, and then drag the gadget near the upper edge of the desktop. Notice that as you move near the top of the desktop, the gadget snaps into position, slightly below the top of the desktop.

Objective 2 | Use the Start Menu and Manage Windows

Some programs and documents are available from the desktop. For most things, however, you will turn to the Start menu. The *Start menu* gives you access to all of the programs on your computer, and also enables you to change the way Windows operates, to access and configure your network, and to get help and support when it is needed. After you have opened several programs, you can rearrange and resize the program windows to fit your needs.

Activity 1.04 | Using the Start Menu

In this activity, you will use the Start menu to open a program, and also to open the Windows Explorer window.

Another Way

Press the Start button on your keyboard—a key with the Windows logo, often found to the left of the spacebar.

1 In the lower left corner of the screen, on the left end of the taskbar, point to and then click the **Start** button 🔵. Compare your screen with Figure 1.17.

The left side of the Start menu contains four areas. At the bottom is the Search box, which enables you to search for files or programs. Above the Search box is the *All Programs* command, which takes you to a list of all of the programs you can access on the computer. *All Programs* displays an arrow, which indicates that a submenu is available for a command. A *submenu* is a second-level menu; the arrow indicates that more items can be found related to the menu command.

Above *All Programs* is an area that contains the most recently opened programs. On the upper left is the *pinned programs area*—an area reserved for programs that you want to display permanently, although you can also remove programs from this area. To remove a program from the pinned list, right-click the program, and then click *Remove from this list*.

On the top of the right side are links to your personal folders, while the bottom sections give you access to computer management features.

Figure 1.17

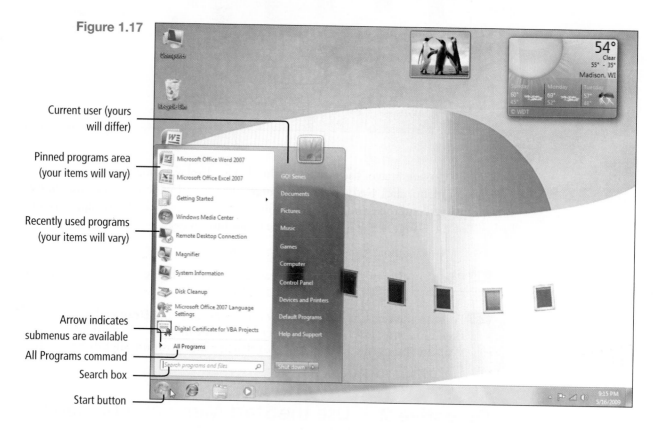

Current user (yours will differ)

Pinned programs area (your items will vary)

Recently used programs (your items will vary)

Arrow indicates submenus are available

All Programs command

Search box

Start button

Alert! | Is your taskbar hidden?

Some computers are set up to hide the taskbar when it is not in use. This adds more workspace to the desktop, and is particularly useful on portable computers with small screens. When the taskbar is hidden, move the pointer to the bottom of the screen, and it will display. However, in this chapter, it is assumed that the taskbar is displayed at all times.

To keep the taskbar displayed on your screen, find an open area on the taskbar, right-click, and then from the shortcut menu, click Properties. In the Taskbar and Start Menu Properties dialog box, on the Taskbar tab, locate the *Auto-hide the taskbar* check box. If the taskbar is hidden, there will be a check mark in the check box. To remove the Auto-hide feature, click the check box one time to clear—remove—the check mark.

2 From the **Start** menu, point to, but do not click, the **All Programs** command. Compare your screen with Figure 1.18.

> The All Programs submenu displays—displaying a portion of the contents found within All Programs—and the *All Programs* command changes to a *Back* command. Your menu will differ from the one shown in Figure 1.18 because your computer will have different programs installed. Folders in the menu contain more programs or more folders or some of each.

Figure 1.18

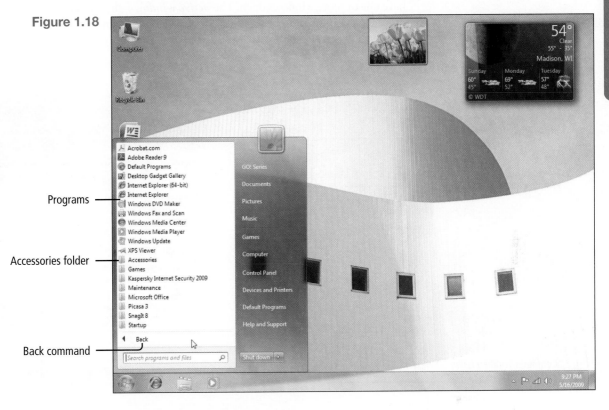

Programs —

Accessories folder —

Back command —

3 Click the **Accessories** folder, and then from the displayed list, click **Calculator**. Notice that the ***window name***—*Calculator*—displays in the title bar.

> The Calculator window opens, and the Start menu closes. You can access the Accessories programs from the Start menu and use them while you are using other programs. For example, you might want to make a quick calculation while you are typing a document in Microsoft Word. You can open the calculator, make the calculation, and then place the result in your Word document without closing Word.

4 Click the **Start** button ⊕ again, and near the middle of the right side of the **Start menu**, click **Computer**. If the Windows Explorer window fills the entire screen, near the right side of the title bar, click the Restore Down button 🗗. Compare your screen with Figure 1.19.

The Windows Explorer window opens, but the Calculator window is either partially or completely hidden, as shown in Figure 1.19. The buttons in the taskbar, however, indicate that two programs are open. The buttons that are outlined indicate the programs that have one or more windows open. The *active window*—the window in which the pointer movements, commands, or text entry occur when two or more windows are open—displays a darker title bar.

Figure 1.19

Darker title bar indicates the active window

Window name in title bar

Computer window hides most of the Calculator window

Calculator window button

Computer window button

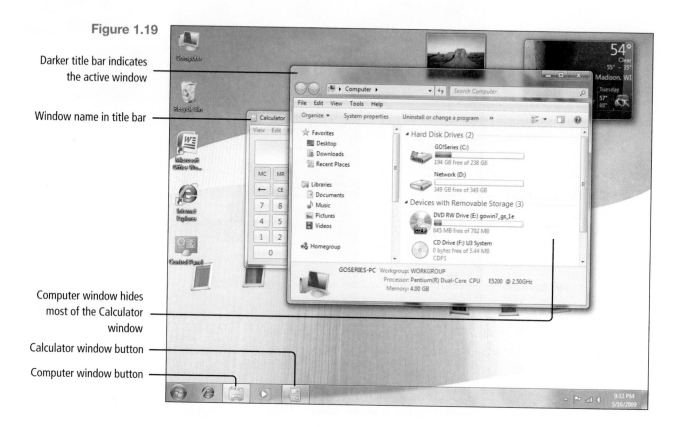

5 Click the **Start** button ⊕, and then click in the **Search programs and files** box. Type **wordpad** and press [Enter]. If the WordPad window fills the entire screen, near the right side of the title bar, click the Restore Down button 🗗.

If you type a program name into the Start menu Search box, the program will open, which enables you to quickly open programs rather than try to find them. *WordPad* is a simple word processing program that comes with Windows 7.

Activity 1.05 | Adding Shortcuts to the Start Menu, Desktop, and Taskbar

There are programs that you will seldom use, and there are programs that you will use all the time. To make frequently used programs easily and quickly available, you can pin a shortcut to the program in the Start menu *pinned programs area*, or you can add a shortcut icon to the desktop or pin the program to the taskbar.

1 Click the **Start** button ⊕, point to **All Programs**, click **Accessories**, and then right-click **Calculator**.

2 From the displayed shortcut menu, click **Pin to Start Menu**. At the bottom of the **Start menu**, click the **Back** button, and notice that *Calculator* has been added to the pinned programs area, as shown in Figure 1.20.

Figure 1.20

Calculator program pinned to Start menu

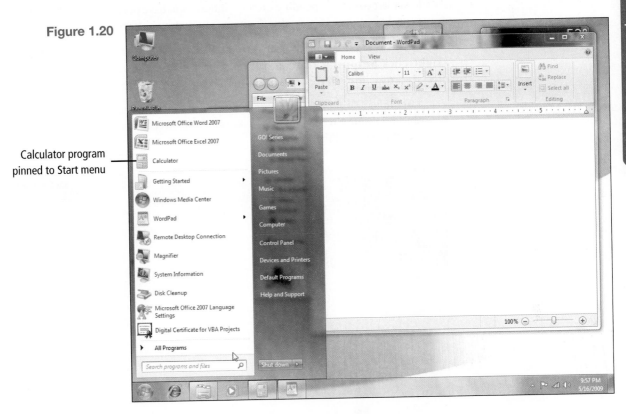

3 Click the **Start** button ⊕, point to **All Programs**, if necessary click **Accessories**, right-click **Calculator**, and then point to—but do not click—**Send to**. Notice the available commands on the *Send to* list, as shown in Figure 1.21.

Figure 1.21

Shortcut menu

Send to command

Desktop (create shortcut) command

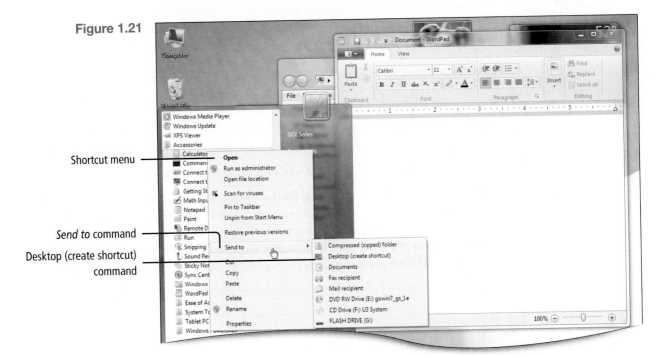

4 From the displayed shortcut menu, click **Desktop (create shortcut)**, and then click in any open area of the desktop.

A Calculator icon is placed on the desktop. The shortcut icon has a small blue arrow in the lower left corner. Depending on the windows you have open, and the number of icons on your desktop, your Calculator shortcut icon may be hidden.

5 Click the **Start** button 🌐, point to **All Programs**, if necessary click **Accessories**, right-click **Snipping Tool**, and then click **Pin to Taskbar**. Click in an open area on the desktop, and then compare your screen with Figure 1.22.

You can use *Snipping Tool* to capture a screen shot, or *snip*, of the entire screen or of any object on your screen, and then make notes on, save, or share the image. You will use this tool throughout this chapter.

Figure 1.22

Calculator shortcut icon added to the desktop

Snipping Tool added to taskbar

6 On the taskbar, click the **Snipping Tool** button ✂️.

The Snipping Tool window displays, and the rest of the screen appears faded.

7 In the **Snipping Tool** window, click the arrow to the right of the **New** button to display a list of potential snips. From the list, click **Full-screen Snip**.

The entire screen is captured, and displays in the Snipping Tool window.

8 Near the top of the **Snipping Tool** window, click the **Save Snip** button 💾. In the **Save As** dialog box, in the left column, click **Desktop** to save the snip to the desktop. In the **File name** box, using your own last and first names, type **Lastname_Firstname_1A_Taskbar** Use the underscore between words—hold down (Shift) and press the dash (-) button to the right of the numbers near the top of the keyboard. Click in the **Save as type** box, and then from the menu, click **JPEG file**. Compare your screen with Figure 1.23.

Figure 1.23

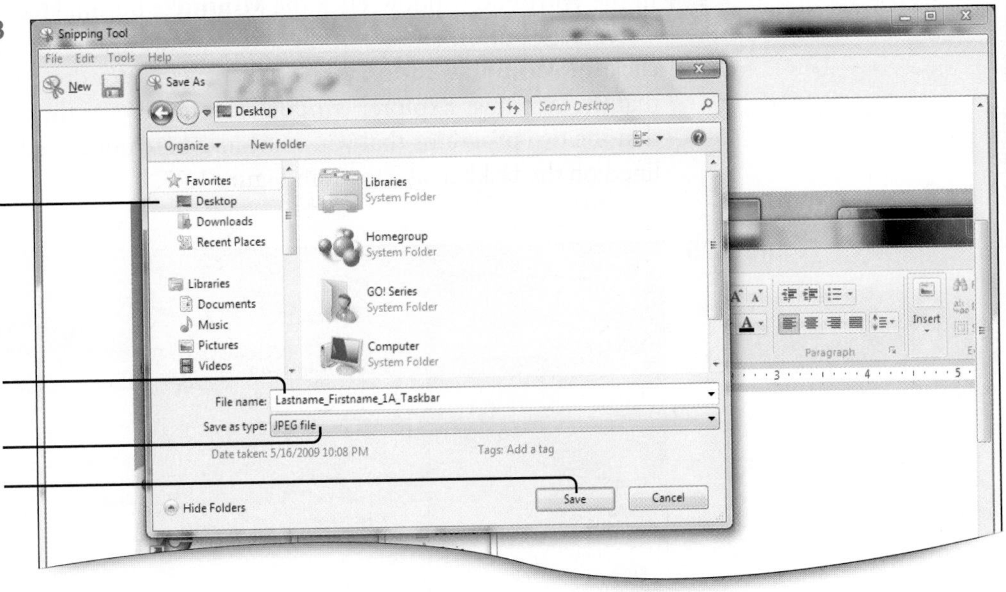

File will be saved on the desktop

File name

File saved in JPEG format

Save button

9 At the bottom of the **Save As** dialog box, click **Save** to save the snip on the desktop.

10 In the upper right corner of the **Snipping Tool** window, click the **Close** button. Notice that your file displays as an icon on the desktop.

Activity 1.06 | Minimizing, Maximizing, and Restoring a Window

You can *maximize* a window, which enlarges the window to occupy the entire screen, and you can *restore* a window, which reduces the window to the size it was before being maximized. You can also *minimize* a window, which reduces the window to a button on the taskbar, removing it from the screen entirely without actually closing it. When you need to view the window again, you can click the taskbar button to bring it back into view.

1 Click anywhere in the **WordPad** window to make it the active window, and then examine the three buttons in the upper right corner of the window. The left button is the **Minimize** button, the middle button is the **Maximize** button, and the right button is the **Close** button.

Another Way

Double-click in the bar at the top of the window.

2 In the **WordPad** window, click the **Maximize** button. Notice that the window expands to cover the entire screen, and the Maximize button changes to a Restore Down button, as shown in Figure 1.24.

Figure 1.24

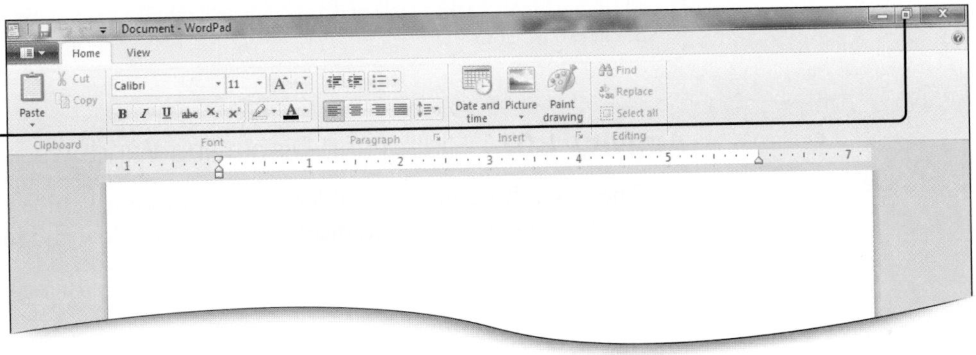

Maximize button changes to Restore Down button

Another Way

Double-click in the
title bar at the top of
the window.

☒ In the **WordPad** window, click the **Restore Down** button 🔲. Notice that the window resumes its former shape, size, and location.

☒ In the **WordPad** window, click the **Minimize** button 🔲. In the taskbar, click the **Calculator** button to make it the active window, and then in the **Calculator** window, click the **Minimize** button 🔲 to display the Windows Explorer window. Notice that the Windows Explorer window now displays as the active window. Notice also that the two programs that you minimized are not closed—their buttons are still outlined on the taskbar, as shown in Figure 1.25.

Figure 1.25

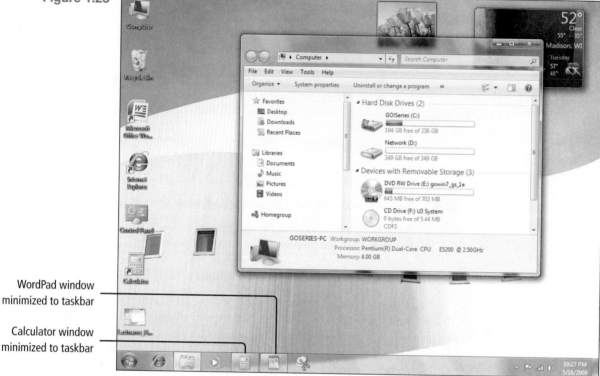

WordPad window
minimized to taskbar

Calculator window
minimized to taskbar

☒ In the taskbar, click the **Calculator** button to restore the Calculator window. Then, click the **WordPad** button to restore the WordPad window.

More Knowledge | Keeping More Than One Program Window Open at a Time

The ability to keep more than one window open at a time will become more useful as you become more familiar with Microsoft Office. For example, if you want to take information from two word processing documents to create a third document, you can open all three documents and use the taskbar to move among them, copying and pasting text from one document to another. Or, you could copy a chart from Excel and paste it into Word or take a table of data and paste it into PowerPoint. You can even have the same document open in two windows.

Activity 1.07 | Hiding and Displaying Windows

There is a shortcut that enables you to temporarily hide all open windows and view the desktop, and also a way to display just one window and hide the rest.

1 Move the pointer to the lower-right corner of the desktop to point to the **Show desktop** button. Notice that all open windows become transparent to give you a *peek* at the desktop—all desktop items display, as shown in Figure 1.26.

This only works if the Aero interface is turned on.

Figure 1.26

Outlines of transparent windows

Show desktop button

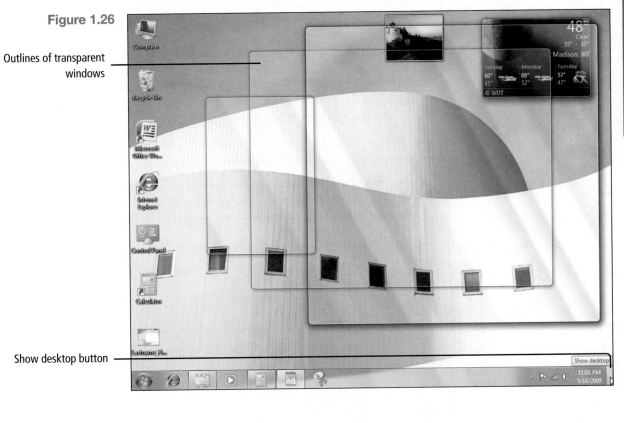

2 Move the pointer away from the **Show desktop** button and notice that the windows display again.

3 Point to the **Show desktop** button, but this time click the button. Notice that all open windows are hidden, and no outlines display.

4 Click the **Show desktop** button again to display all open windows.

5 In the taskbar, locate and click the **Calculator** button to make the Calculator the active window. Notice that the background of the Calculator icon on the taskbar is brighter than the icons for the other open windows.

6 Point to the **Calculator** title bar, hold down the left mouse button, and then *shake*—move the window back and forth quickly—the window.

All windows except the shaken window are hidden.

7 Shake the **Calculator** window again to display all of the open windows.

Objective 3 | Resize, Move, and Scroll Windows

When a window opens on your screen, it generally opens in the same size and shape as it was when last used. If you are using more than one window at a time, you can increase or decrease the size of a window, or move a window so that you can see the information you need.

As you work within a program, the information you create will likely grow larger than the screen can display. When the information in a window extends beyond the right or lower edges of the window, scroll bars display at the bottom and right. Using the *horizontal scroll bar*, you can move left and right to view information that extends beyond the left or right edge of the screen. Using the *vertical scroll bar*, you can move up and down to view information that extends beyond the top or bottom of the screen.

Activity 1.08 │ Customizing and Using the Taskbar

When you have a number of windows open, you can use the taskbar to quickly review the contents of each document to determine which one to use. You can also move the taskbar to the top, left, or right edges of the desktop.

1 On the taskbar, point to—but do not click—the **Windows Explorer** button ⬛, and then compare your screen with Figure 1.27.

> A thumbnail of the window displays. A *thumbnail* is a miniature representation of a window or a file. If two documents are open in the same program, two thumbnails will display. The Aero interface must be turned on for this feature to work.

Figure 1.27

Thumbnail of the
Computer window

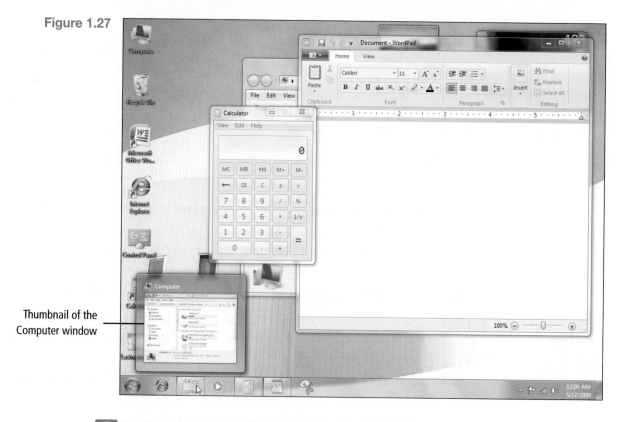

2 On the taskbar, point to—but do not click—the **Calculator** button. Move the pointer and point to the **WordPad** button.

3 Click the **Start** button ⬤, point to **All Programs**, click **Accessories**, and then click **Paint**.

If the Paint window is maximized, click the Restore Down button ⬜.

> *Paint* is a simple drawing program that comes with Windows 7. Four programs are now open, and there are icons on the taskbar for other unopened programs, such as Snipping Tool.

4 Hold down the [Alt] key, and then press the [Tab] key. Compare your screen with Figure 1.28.

> The screen displays thumbnails of the windows that are open, including the desktop; if the Aero interface is not turned on, only the program icons display.

Figure 1.28

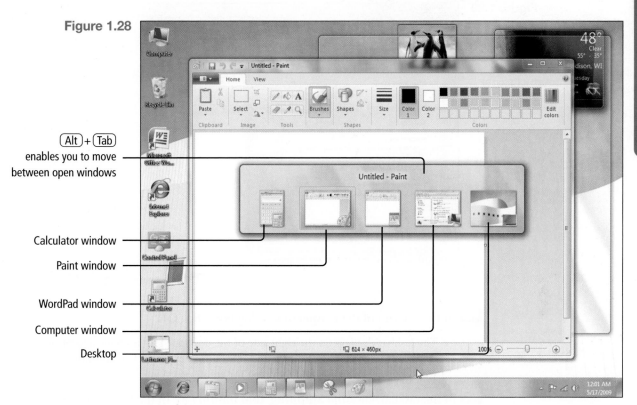

[Alt] + [Tab] enables you to move between open windows

Calculator window

Paint window

WordPad window

Computer window

Desktop

5 Continue to hold down [Alt], but press [Tab] several times. Notice that the selected window moves from left to right in the list of thumbnails.

> When you release the [Alt] key, the window in the active thumbnail becomes the active window on the desktop.

6 Move to the **Calculator** window, and then release the [Alt] button.

7 On the taskbar, point to the **Windows Explorer** window, and then right-click.

> A *jump list* displays frequent destinations you might want to jump to from the Windows Explorer window. If you display a jump list for a program such as a word processor or a spreadsheet, a list of recently edited files also displays, enabling you to quickly open any desired files.

8 Right-click an open area of the taskbar, and then from the shortcut menu, click **Properties**.

9 In the **Properties** dialog box, be sure the Taskbar tab is selected. Under **Taskbar appearance**, click the **Taskbar location on screen arrow**, and then click **Right**. Compare your screen with Figure 1.29.

Figure 1.29

Taskbar tab ————

Screen location of the taskbar ————

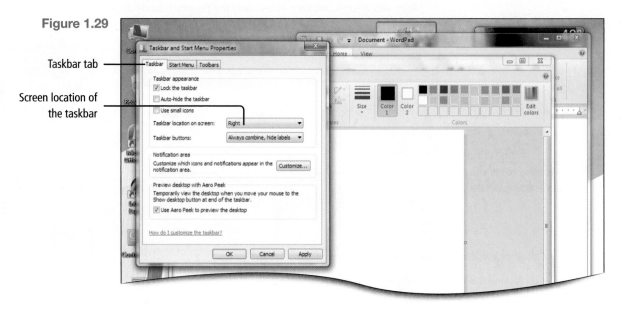

10 At the bottom of the **Properties** dialog box, click **OK**.

The taskbar displays on the right side of the desktop. This is an ideal location if you are using a widescreen monitor or a portable computer with a wide monitor because it gives you more vertical space on the screen for your documents.

11 In the taskbar, click the **Snipping Tool** button. In the **Snipping Tool** window, click the arrow to the right of the **New** button to display a list of potential snips. From the list, click **Full-screen Snip**.

12 Near the top of the **Snipping Tool** window, click the **Save Snip** button. In the **Save As** dialog box, in the left column, click **Desktop**. In the **File name** box, using your own last and first names, type **Lastname_Firstname_1A_Windows** Click in the **Save as type** box and be sure **JPEG file** is selected.

13 At the bottom of the **Save As** dialog box, click **Save** to save the snip on the desktop.

14 In the upper right corner of the **Snipping Tool** window, click the **Close** button. Notice that your file displays as an icon on the desktop.

15 Use the procedure you practiced in Steps 8 through 10 to return the taskbar to the bottom of the desktop.

Activity 1.09 | Resizing, Moving, Scrolling, and Closing Windows

In the following activity, you will resize and move the Windows Explorer window. You will also use the vertical scroll bar in the window to view information that does not fit in the window.

1 On the right end of the taskbar, click the **Show desktop** button to hide all of the windows.

2 On the taskbar, click the **Windows Explorer** button to display the Windows Explorer window.

3 Move the pointer to the lower right corner of the window to display the diagonal resize pointer, and then compare your screen with Figure 1.30.

When the mouse pointer is in this shape, you can use it to change the size and shape of a window.

Figure 1.30

Diagonal resize pointer

Show desktop button

4 Hold down the left mouse button, ***drag***—move the mouse while holding down the left mouse button and then release at the appropriate time—diagonally up and to the left until you see a scroll bar at the right side of the window, and then release the mouse button. Adjust as necessary so that the Windows Explorer window is the approximate size of the one shown in Figure 1.31.

Notice that a vertical scroll bar displays on the right side of the window, and another one displays on the right side of the Navigation pane. A scroll bar is added to the window whenever the window contains more than it can display.

Figure 1.31

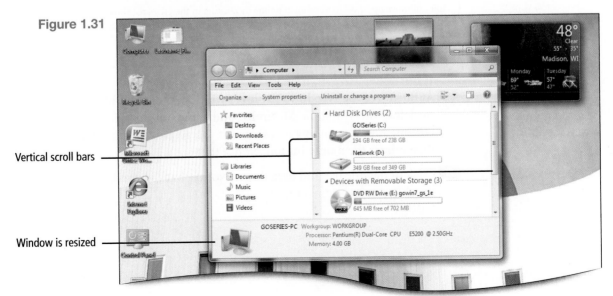

Vertical scroll bars

Window is resized

5 In the **Windows Explorer** window **file list**, at the bottom of the vertical scroll bar, point to the **down arrow** ▼ and click two times. Notice that information at the bottom of the window scrolls up so that you can see the information that was not visible before, as shown in Figure 1.32.

Figure 1.32

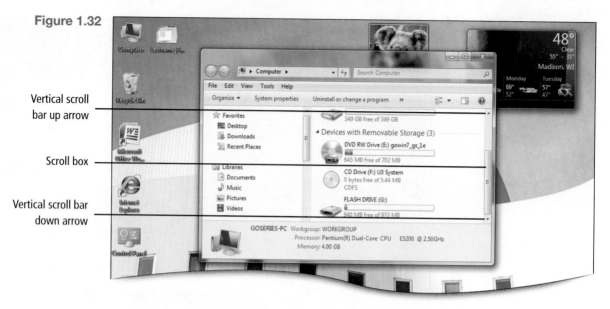

Vertical scroll bar up arrow

Scroll box

Vertical scroll bar down arrow

6 On the same scroll bar, point to the **up arrow** ▲, and then click and hold down the left mouse button.

The window scrolls to the top of the file list. You can click and hold down the left mouse button on the up or down scroll arrows to scroll rapidly through a long list of information.

7 Point to the scroll box, and then drag it downward.

The *scroll box* displays within the vertical and horizontal scroll bars and provides a visual indication of your location within the information displayed. It can also be used with the mouse to reposition the information on the screen. Moving the scroll box gives you more control as you scroll because you can see the information as it moves up or down in the window.

Note | Moving a Screen at a Time

You can move up or down a screen at a time by clicking in the gray area above or below the vertical scroll box. You can also move left or right a screen at a time by clicking in the area to the left or right of a horizontal scroll box. The size of the scroll box indicates the relative size of the display to the whole document. If the scroll box is small, it means that the display is a small portion of the entire document.

---

8 At the top of the **Windows Explorer** window, point to a blank area in the title bar to the left of the Minimize, Maximize, and Close buttons. Hold down the left mouse button, drag the window up as far as it will go past the top edge of the window, and then release the mouse button. Notice that the window is maximized.

9 Click in the title bar and drag down. Notice that the window is restored to its original size, but not its original location.

10 In the **Windows Explorer** window title bar, click the **Close** button [x]. In the taskbar, right-click the **Paint** button [icon], and then click **Close window**. Use the same technique to close the **Calculator** window [icon].

11 In the taskbar, click the **WordPad** button to display the WordPad window. Using the title bar, drag the WordPad window to the right edge of the desktop until it changes shape to occupy the right half of the desktop, and then release the mouse button.

> You can use this method to open two windows side by side if you drag a second window to the left border.

12 Click in the WordPad window, type your first and last names, and then press [Enter]. Locate the **Lastname_Firstname_1A_Taskbar** icon on the desktop—you may have to click the two snip files to find the correct file.

13 Drag the **Lastname_Firstname_1A_Taskbar** file to the line below your name in the WordPad document, and then release the mouse button. Compare your screen with Figure 1.33.

> The contents of the file you dragged are pasted into the WordPad document.

Figure 1.33

Your name

File dragged into WordPad document

File icon

14 Drag the **Lastname_Firstname_1A_Windows** file to the line below the figure you just inserted into the WordPad document. In the WordPad title bar, click the **Save** button [icon].

15 In the **Save As** dialog box, in the **Navigation** pane, click **Desktop**. In the **File name** box, type **Lastname_Firstname_1A_WordPad** and then click **Save**.

16 If you are to print your document, hold down [Ctrl] and then press [P] to display the Print dialog box. Be sure the correct printer is selected, and then click **Print**. If you are to submit this document electronically, follow your instructor's directions.

17 **Close** [x] the WordPad window.

End **You have completed Project 1A** ⎯⎯⎯⎯⎯⎯⎯⎯⎯⎯⎯

Project 1B Manage Files and Folders

In Activities 1.10 through 1.18 you will create folders, and then copy, move, rename, and delete files and folders. You will add tags to files and use the Windows 7 search features to search for files. Your screens will look similar to those in Figure 1.34.

Project Files

For Project 1B, you will need the following files:

36 sample files, and two folders containing 14 additional files

You will save your documents as:

Lastname_Firstname_1B_Renamed_Folder
Lastname_Firstname_1B_Compressed_Folder
Lastname_Firstname_1B_Search_Folder

Project Results

Figure 1.34

Objective 4 | Create, Move, and Rename Folders

Information that you create in a computer program is stored in the computer's memory, which is a temporary storage location. This data will be lost if the computer is turned off. To keep the information you create, you must save it as a file on one of the drives available to you. For example, a five-page term paper that you create in a word processing program such as Microsoft Word, when saved, is a *file*. Files can be stored directly on a drive, but more commonly are stored in a folder on the drive. A *folder* is a container for programs and files, represented on the screen by a picture of a common paper file folder.

Use folders to organize your files so that you can easily locate them for later use. Folders and files must be created and stored on one of the drives attached to your computer. Your available drives fall into three categories: 1) the nonremovable hard drive, also called the *local disk*, inside the computer; 2) removable drives that you insert into the computer, such as a flash drive, an external hard drive, or a writable CD or DVD; or 3) a shared network drive connected to your computer through a computer network, such as the network at your college.

Activity 1.10 | Opening and Navigating Windows Explorer

Windows Explorer is a program that enables you to create and manage folders, and copy, move, sort, and delete files. In the following activity, you will create a folder on one of the three types of drives available to you—the local disk (hard drive), a removable drive (USB flash drive, an external hard drive, or some other type of removable drive), or a network drive. If you are using a computer in a college lab, you may have space assigned to you on a shared network drive. You can create these folders on any drive that is available to you. For the rest of this chapter, a flash drive will be used.

1 On the taskbar, click the **Windows Explorer** button 🖿. If this button is not available, click the **Start** button 🌐, point to All Programs, click Accessories, and then click Windows Explorer.

> The Windows Explorer window opens, with the Navigation pane displayed on the left, and the Libraries pane displayed on the right. You may also see a Details pane just above the taskbar and a Preview pane on the right side of the window.

More Knowledge | Using Libraries

Libraries are folders used to sort files with similar content. By default, Windows 7 sets up four libraries: Documents, Music, Pictures, and Videos. Each of these libraries is assigned two folders—a user folder and a public folder. For example, the Documents library contains the My Documents subfolder for the current user, along with the Public Documents subfolder on the hard disk, which contains files that can be shared with all users. If you have other fixed drives on your computer, or permanent network drives, you can add other folders to a library so that all files of a similar type can be accessed quickly using the library.

Another Way

On the right side of the title bar, click the Maximize button 🔲.

2 If the window is not maximized, drag the title bar to the top of the screen.

3 On the Command bar, click the **Organize** button, and then point to **Layout**. If the Details pane does not display at the bottom of your window, click Details Pane. If the Navigation pane does not display on the left side of your window, repeat the procedure and click Navigation Pane. Compare your screen with Figure 1.35.

Figure 1.35

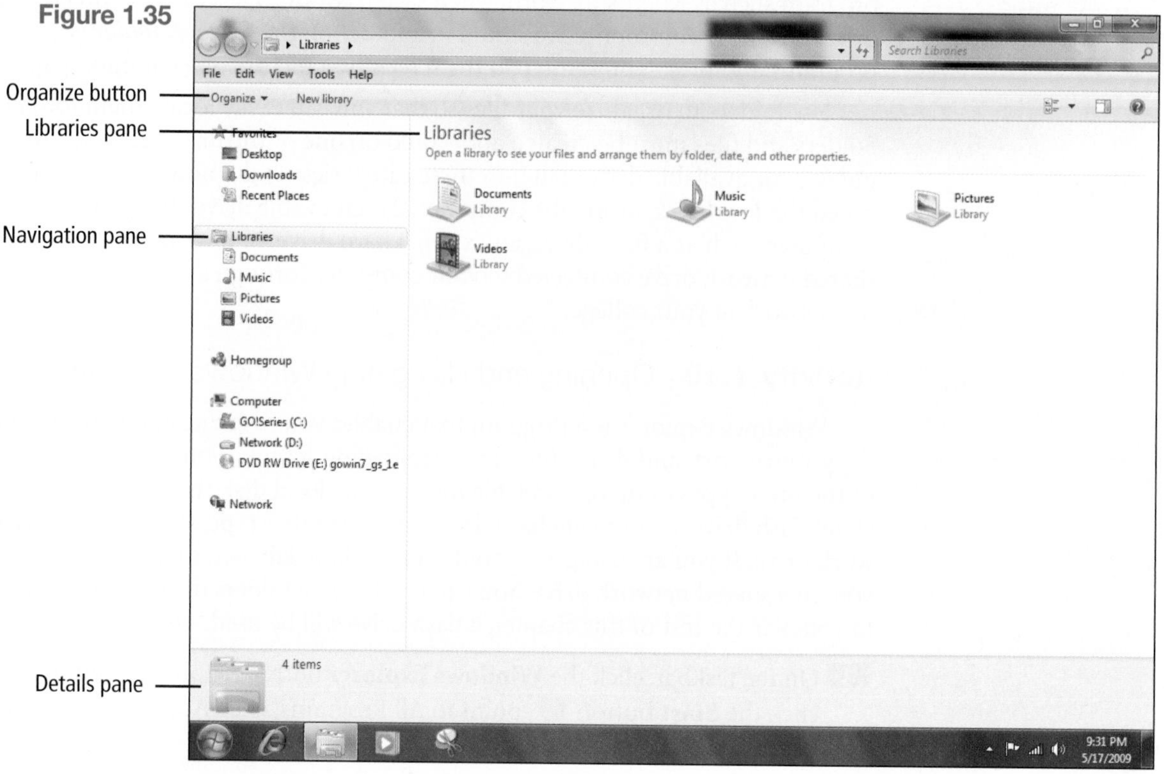

Organize button —
Libraries pane —
Navigation pane —

Details pane —

4 In the **Navigation** pane, if necessary scroll down, and then click **Computer**.

The file list displays a list of hard drives, removable storage devices, network drives, and other devices connected to the computer.

5 In the **Navigation** pane, if necessary, to the left of **Computer**, click the open arrow ▷. Notice that the arrow changes to a filled arrow pointing downward at an angle ◢.

The open arrow indicates that there are other folders and drives to be displayed. When you click the open arrow, the next level of folders and drives displays. The list of drives in the Navigation pane matches the list of drives in the file list.

6 Insert your USB flash drive or other removable drive. If an AutoPlay dialog box displays asking what you want Windows to do, click the Close button. In the **Navigation** pane, under **Computer**, click your removable drive—for this chapter, the removable drive name will be FLASH DRIVE (G:); yours will be different.

7 Compare your screen with Figure 1.36. Notice that the file list in the figure is empty; your storage device or drive may already contain files and folders.

Figure 1.36

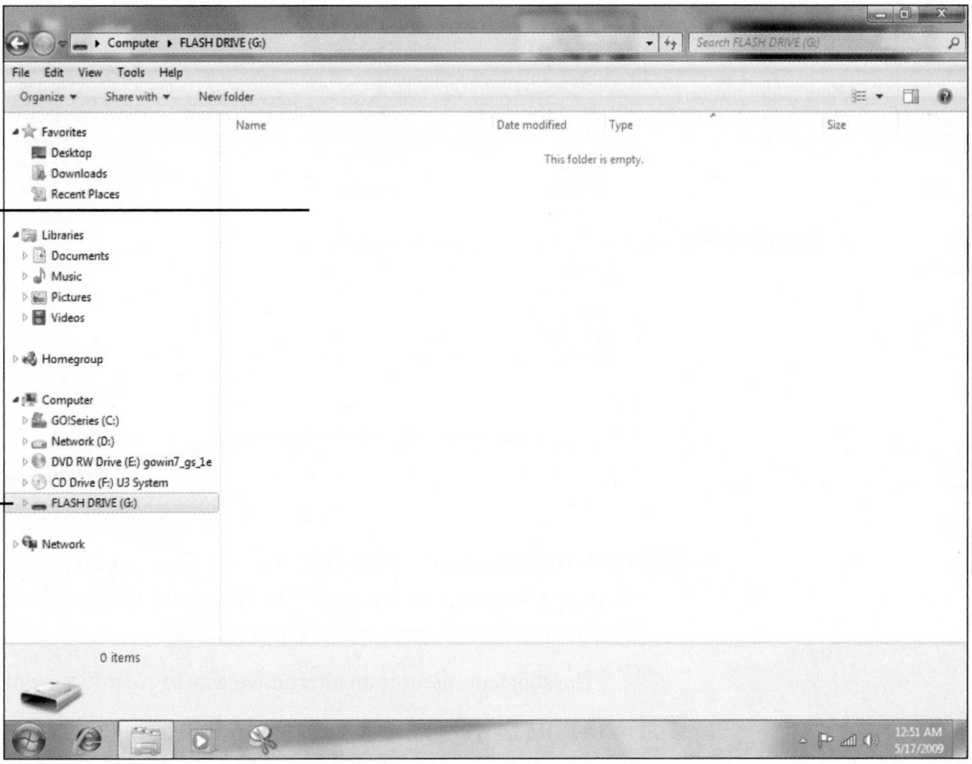

File list is empty; yours may have files and folders

Flash drive (your drive name and letter will vary)

More Knowledge | Computer Storage Devices

The hard drive (local disk) is usually identified on your computer by the notation C: (and sometimes D:, E:, and so on for additional drives). *Flash drives*—also known as *USB drives* or *thumb drives*—are small storage devices that plug into a computer's Universal Serial Bus (USB) port, which provides a connection between a computer and a peripheral device such as a printer, a mouse, a keyboard, or a USB drive.

You may also have access to files on another type of storage device, a *CD*—Compact Disc, or a *DVD*—Digital Video (or Versatile) Disc. CD and DVD drives are optical storage devices that come in two formats—read-only and read-write. If you are using files stored on a read-only CD or a DVD disc, you will need to open a file from the disc, and then save it to a writable drive, or copy a file to another disk and then open it.

Activity 1.11 | Creating a New Folder

It is always a good idea to create a new folder when you have a new category of files to store. You do not need to create a new folder for each type of file, however. You can store many different kinds of files in the same folder.

Another Way

If you accidentally press Enter before you have a chance to name the folder, you can still rename it. Right-click the folder, click Rename from the shortcut menu, type a new name, and then press Enter.

1 With the flash drive selected, in the Command bar, click the **New folder** button.

A new folder—named *New folder*—is created with the name of the folder displayed in the *edit mode*. Edit mode enables you to change the name of a file or folder, and works the same in all Windows programs.

2 With *New Folder* selected, substitute your name where indicated, and type **Pictures of Firstname Lastname** and then press ⏎. Click anywhere in the blank area of the file list to deselect the new folder and compare your screen with Figure 1.37.

Figure 1.37

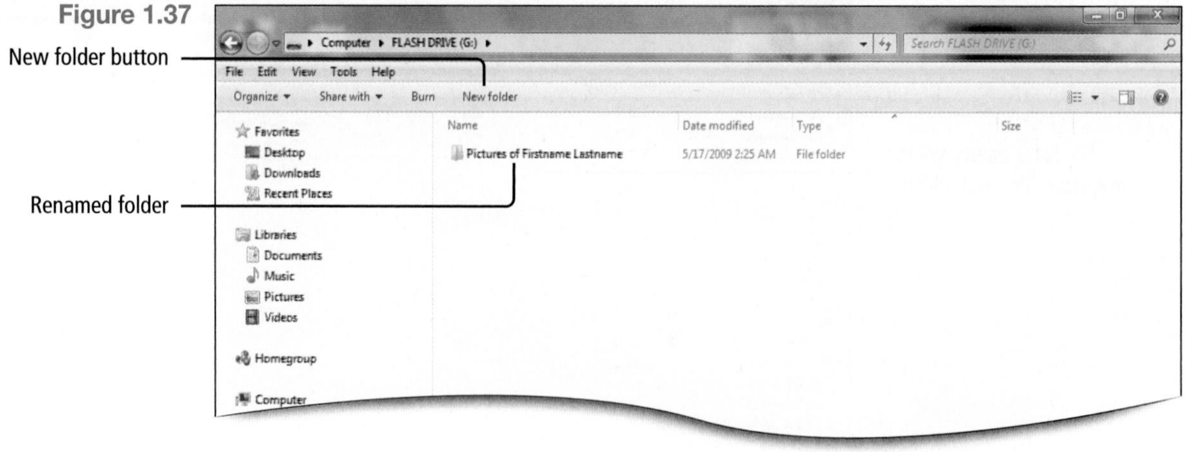

New folder button

Renamed folder

3 With the removable drive still selected, in an open area of the **file list**, right-click to display a shortcut menu, point to **New**, and then click **Folder**. Type **Documents of Firstname Lastname** and then press ⏎.

The shortcut menu is an alternative way to create a new folder.

4 In the **file list**, click the **Name** column heading several times to sort the folders and file names from *a* to *z* and from *z* to *a*. Notice that the arrow in the Name column heading points up when the folders are displayed in *ascending order* (*a* to *z*), and points down when the folders are displayed in *descending order* (*z* to *a*). Stop when the folders are sorted in descending alphabetical order—from *z* to *a*.

5 In the **file list**, move the pointer to the line at the right of the **Name** column heading to display the resize pointer ✥, as shown in Figure 1.38. Drag the resize pointer ✥ to the right or left to make the column slightly wider than the longest folder name.

Figure 1.38

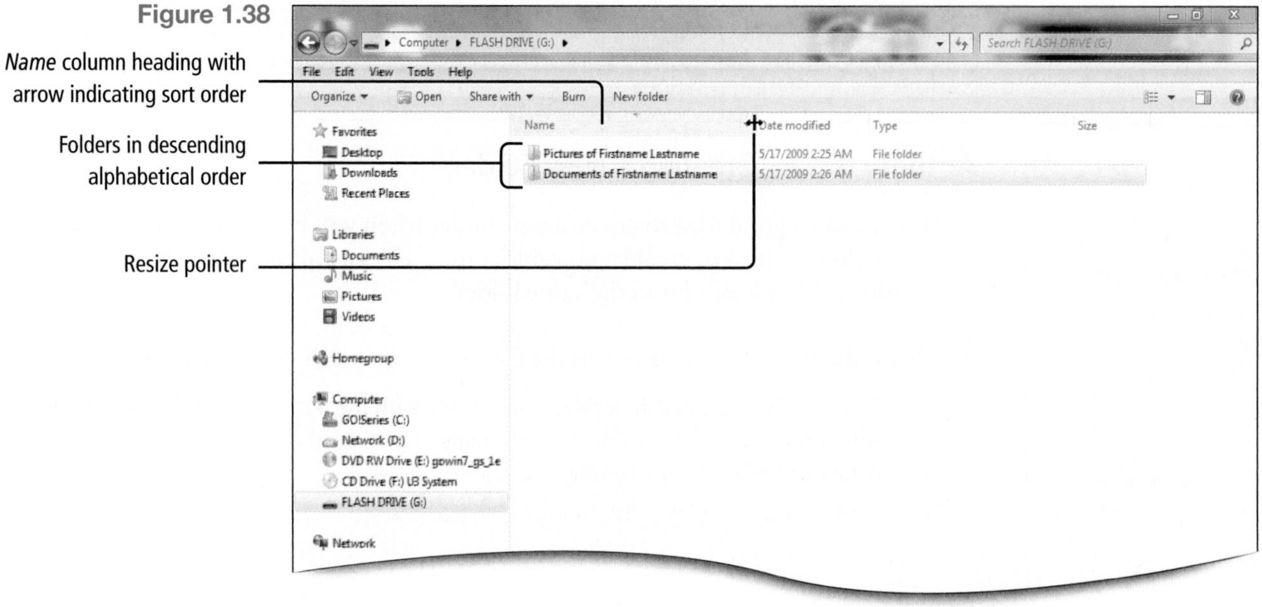

Name column heading with arrow indicating sort order

Folders in descending alphabetical order

Resize pointer

Activity 1.12 | Moving and Renaming Folders

Your student files and folders for this book are stored on a CD or another location chosen by your instructor. You can move the folders, including the files in the folders, from another location to your flash drive or other storage device.

1 Navigate to the location where your student files for this book are stored. They may be stored on a CD, in a course management system, on a hard drive, or on a shared network drive. In this chapter, the data CD is used.

2 In the **Navigation** pane, on the data CD, click the open arrow ▷ to display the folder on the disc. Click the **01_student_data_files** folder, and then compare your screen with Figure 1.39. If your files and folders do not display the way they display in the figure, on the Command bar, to the right of the *Change your view* button, click the *More options* arrow, and then click Details.

There are two folders and a number of files in this folder. The total number of files and folders is displayed in the Details pane at the bottom of the screen. There are more files in the two folders, but they are not included in the totals in the Details pane—only the files and the folders currently displayed in the file list are counted.

Figure 1.39

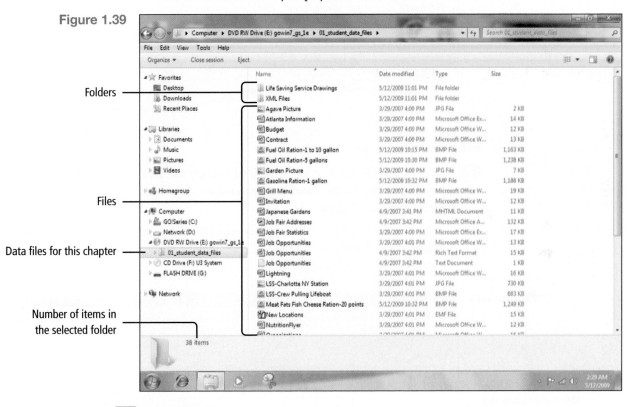

Folders

Files

Data files for this chapter

Number of items in the selected folder

3 In the **file list**, move the pointer to the right border of the **Name** column heading to display the ⬌ pointer. Double-click to resize the border to the widest folder or file name. Repeat this procedure to display the full **Date modified** and **Type** column contents.

Note | Changing the Columns that Display in the File List

If one or more of the columns displayed in Figure 1.39 do not display, right-click anywhere in the file list column titles, and then click the desired column.

---

4 In the **Navigation** pane, if necessary, click the open arrow ▷ to the left of your flash drive. Be sure your student files and folders from the data CD still display in the file list.

5 Near the top of the **file list**, locate the **XML Files** folder. Click on the folder, hold the mouse button down, and drag the folder to the **Navigation** pane directly on top of your storage drive, as shown in Figure 1.40. Notice that a folder displays attached to the pointer, and a ScreenTip says *Copy to FLASH DRIVE (G:)*—your folder or drive name will vary.

Figure 1.40

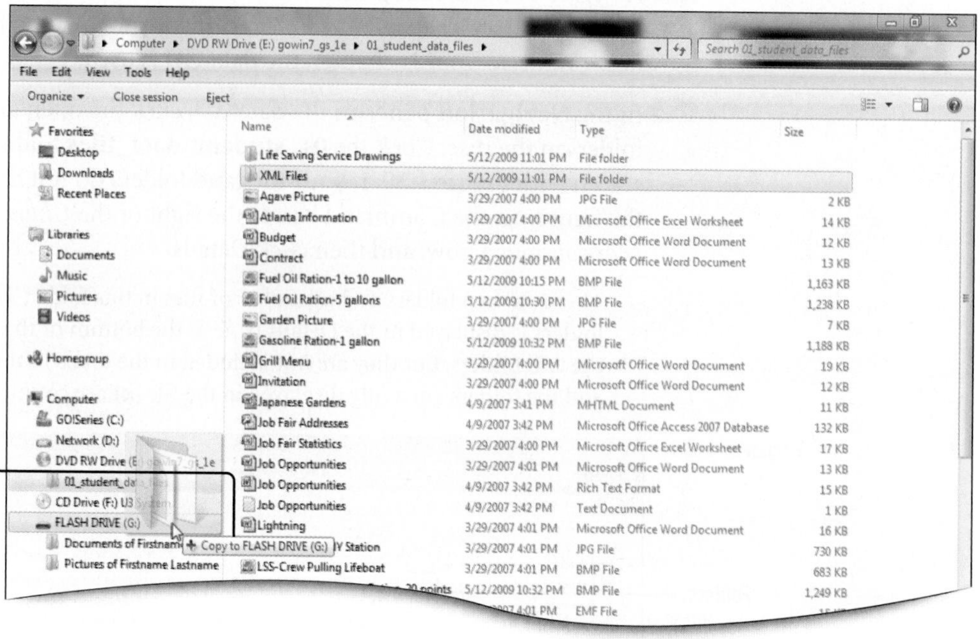

ScreenTip indicates copy location

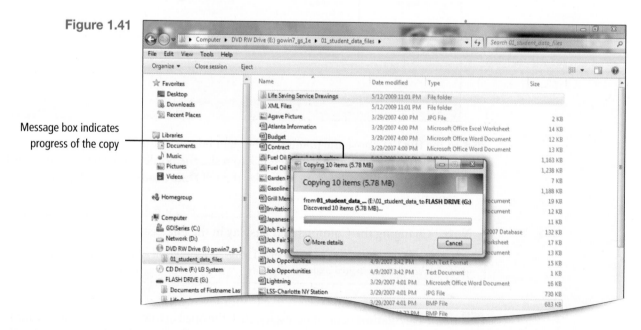

6 Release the mouse button.

7 Repeat the procedure you just practiced to copy the **Life Saving Service Drawings** folder to your flash drive, and notice that a message box indicates the progress of the copy, as shown in Figure 1.41.

The message box displays because the size of the *Life Saving Service Drawings* folder is much larger than the size of the *XML Files* folder and takes a few seconds to copy. The original files remain on the CD.

Figure 1.41

Message box indicates progress of the copy

8 In the **Navigation** pane, click the flash drive or other device where you are storing your files and folders. In the **file list**, right-click the **Life Saving Service Drawings** folder, and then from the displayed shortcut menu, click **Rename**.

9 With the folder name in edit mode, type **LSS Drawings** and then press Enter.

The folder name is changed. When text is selected, typing replaces all of the selected text.

10 Use the skills you practiced earlier to create a **Full-screen Snip**. Click the **Save Snip** button. In the **Save As** dialog box, in the left pane, scroll down to display the **Computer** drives. Click your flash drive, and then in the Command bar, click the **New folder** button. Name the new folder **Windows Chapter 1** Press Enter, and then press Enter again to open the new folder. In the **File name** box, type **Lastname_Firstname_1B_Renamed_Folder** Click **Save**, and then **Close** the Snipping Tool window.

Objective 5 | Copy, Move, Rename, and Delete Files

Copying files from one folder to another is a frequent data management task. For example, you might want to make a backup copy of important information, copy a file from a CD to a local disk, or copy information from your local disk drive to a removable drive. Copying files works the same regardless of the type of drive.

Performing other operations on files, such as deleting them or moving them, also works the same regardless of the type of drive. As you accumulate files, you will likely need to delete some to reduce clutter on your hard drive. You might also want to move documents into other folders on another drive to *archive* them—place them somewhere for long-term storage. Finally, you may want to change the names of file to make the names more descriptive. All of these tasks are functions of your Windows 7 operating system.

Activity 1.13 | Copying Files

1 In the **Navigation** pane, under **Computer**, scroll to the location where your student data files for this book are stored. Locate and click the folder named **01_student_data_files** to display the files and folders in the folder.

2 In the **Navigation** pane, scroll as necessary to display your flash drive or other storage device. Be sure your student data files and folders still display in the file list.

3 Near the middle of the **file list**, locate the **Garden Picture** file, and then drag it to your storage device. Recall that dragging also includes releasing the mouse button at the destination location.

When you drag a file or folder from one device to another, it is copied, which means that the original file remains on the original drive and a copy of the file is placed on the new drive. If you drag a file or folder to another place (such as a folder) on the same drive—for example, from one folder to another—the file or folder is moved and no longer resides in the original location.

4 Locate the **Grill Menu** file, right-click the file, and then click **Copy**.

This creates a copy of the Grill Menu file and places it in a temporary storage area called the *Clipboard*. Files in the Clipboard can be placed in other folders using the Paste command.

5 In the **Navigation** pane, click your storage device. In the **file list**, right-click in an open area, and then from the shortcut menu, click **Paste**. Notice that the file is copied to the open folder.

6 Click the **Name** column heading as necessary to sort the folders in ascending order—the arrow in the column heading should be pointing up. Compare your screen with Figure 1.42.

> The file list should display five folders—the three that you created and the two that you copied. In addition, the two files that you copied should display below the folders. When you sort a folder in ascending order, the folders always display first.

Figure 1.42

Folders display first ⟶

Folders and files sorted in alphabetical order by Name ⟶

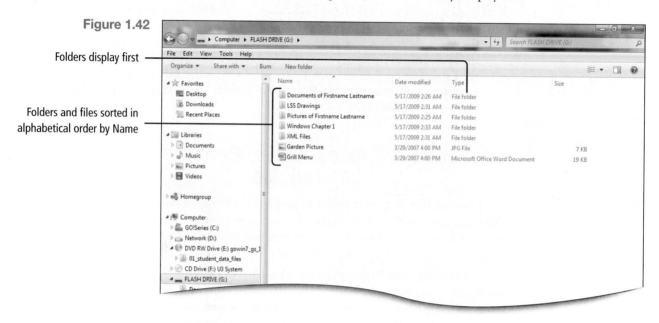

7 Display the files and folders in the **01_student_data_files** folder again. Click the **Atlanta Information** file, hold down [Shift], and then click the **Fuel Oil Ration-1 to 10 gallon** file.

> By holding down the Shift key, you select the two files you click and all of the files in between.

8 In the **Navigation** pane, scroll as necessary to display your storage area. Drag the selected files to your storage area.

9 Click the **Agave Picture** file, hold down [Ctrl], and then click the **Fuel Oil Ration-5 gallons** file, and then the **Gasoline Ration-1 gallon** file. Notice that by using the Control key, you can select several files that are not next to each other, as shown in Figure 1.43.

Figure 1.43

Selected files ⟶

10 Drag the selected files to your storage area.

11 In the **file list**, click the **Invitation** file, and then use the vertical scroll bar to scroll to the bottom of the file list. Hold down Shift, and then click the **Volunteers** file. In the Detail area, notice that the number of files displays, as shown in Figure 1.44. If the total size of the files does not display, in the Details pane, click Show more details.

Figure 1.44

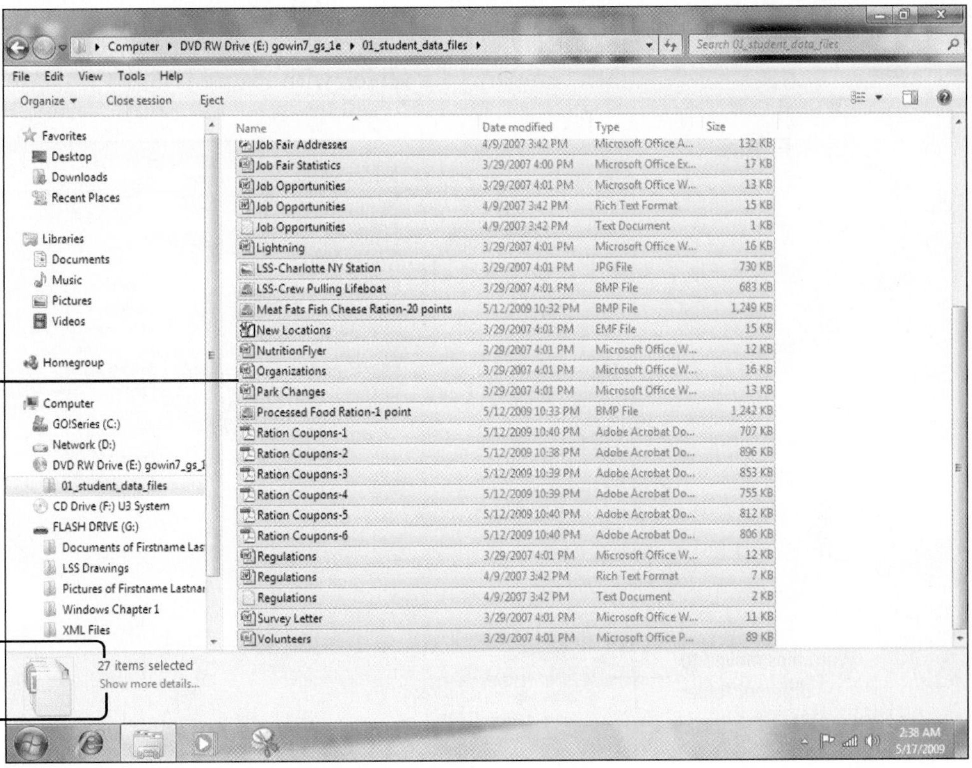

Selected files ⟶

Click to show more details ⟶

Show more details
command ⟶

12 Drag the selected files to your storage area.

More Knowledge | File Extensions

The files you see may display three or four letters following the file name, such as *.docx*. These are *file extensions*, and most files have these extensions—although they may or may not display on your system. Files created by Microsoft Office programs have a standard set of extensions that identify the type of program used to create the file. For example, Microsoft Word documents end in *.doc* or *.docx*, Excel worksheets end in *.xls* or *.xlsx*, PowerPoint presentations end with *.ppt* or *pptx*, and so on. The default setting in Windows 7 is to hide the file extensions.

Activity 1.14 | Moving, Renaming, and Deleting Files

In the following activity, you will move files from one location on your removable drive to another location on the same drive. You will also rename and delete files.

1 In the **Navigation** pane, scroll as necessary and then click on your flash drive or other storage device.

Your storage device should display five folders at the top, and a total of 36 files in the drive—41 objects, as displayed in the Details pane.

2 In the **file list**, click the **Type** column header to sort the files by file type. Move the pointer to the right border of the **Type** column heading to display the ⟷ pointer. Double-click to resize the border to the widest file type.

3 In the **file list**, use the wheel in the middle of your mouse, or the vertical scroll bar, to scroll down until you can see all of the **Microsoft Office Word Document** files.

4 Click the **Budget** file, hold down Shift, and then click the **Survey Letter** file to select all of the Word documents. Drag the selected files to the **Documents of Firstname Lastname** folder.

The files are moved to the new folder, and no longer display in their original location.

5 In the **Navigation** pane, click the **Documents of Firstname Lastname** folder, and then compare your screen with Figure 1.45.

Figure 1.45

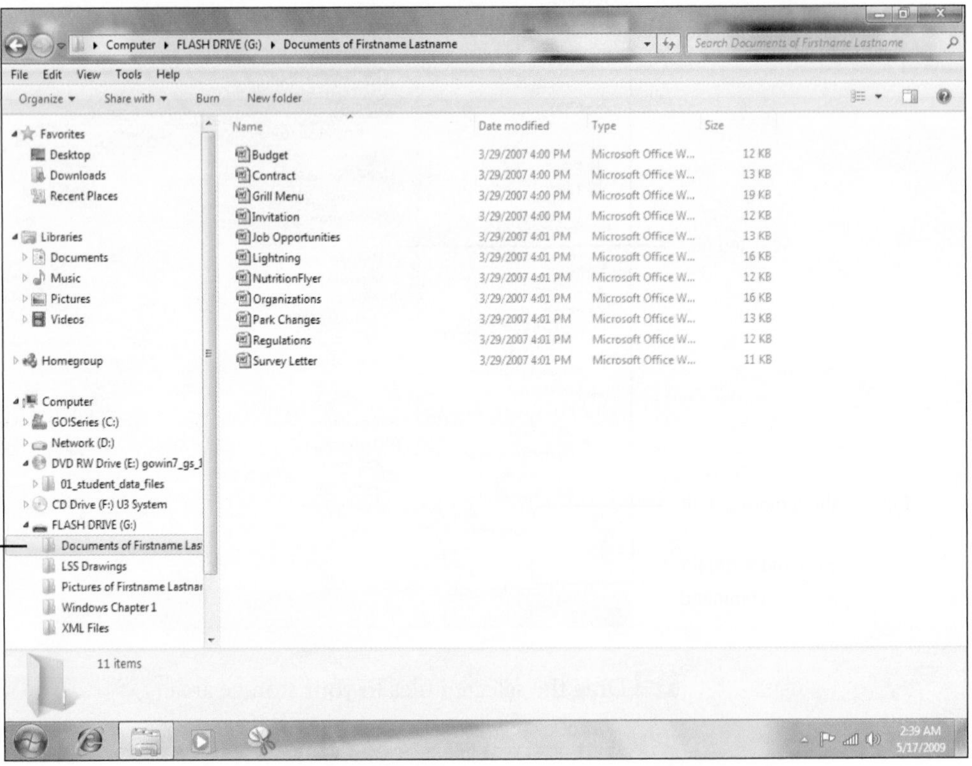

Word files moved to different folder

6 In the **Navigation** pane, click on your flash drive or other storage device. Using the technique you just practiced, select the three **JPG Images**, and then drag them to the **Pictures of Firstname Lastname** folder.

Alert! | What if your file types differ?

Files can be associated with several different programs, and will display a different file type in the Type column. For example, the three files labeled JPG in Figure 1.46 could be called JPEG files on your computer.

---

7 Select the six **BMP Files** and drag them to the **Pictures of Firstname Lastname** folder. If you do not see files labeled *BMP File*, select the six files beginning with *Fuel Oil Ration-1 to 10 gallon* and ending with *Processed Food Ration-1 point.*

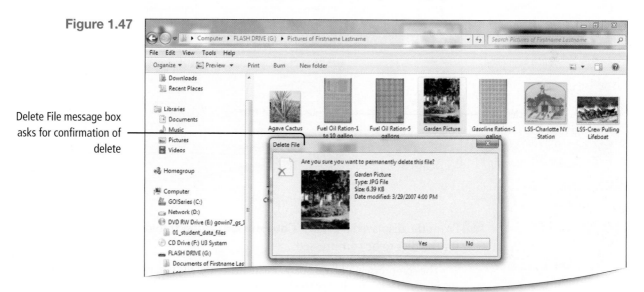

8 In the **Navigation** pane, click the **Pictures of Firstname Lastname** folder, and then compare your screen with Figure 1.46.

Figure 1.46

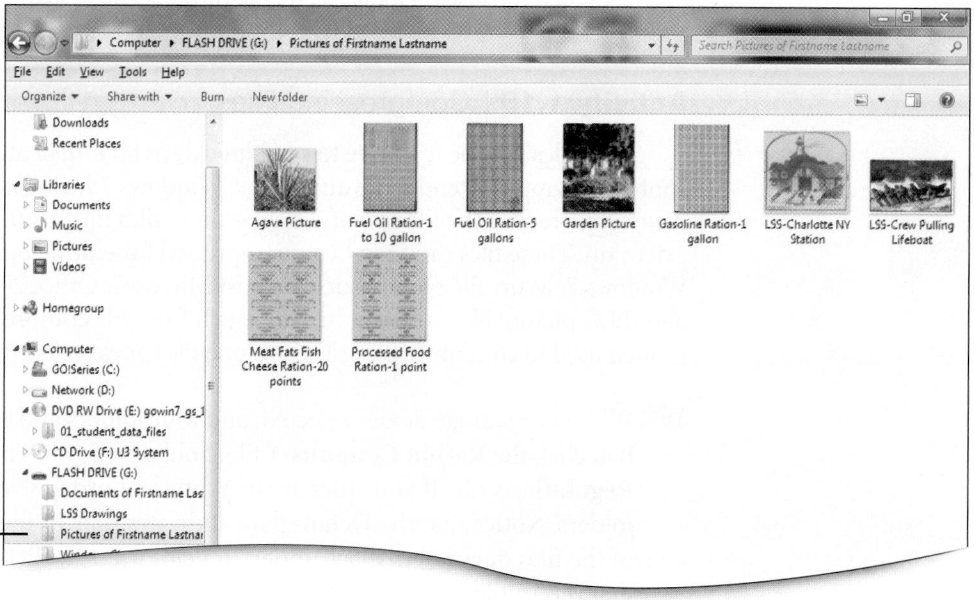

Picture files moved to new folder

9 If thumbnails do not display for the files, on the Command bar, to the right of the **Change your view** button, click the **More options arrow**, and then click **Large Icons**.

10 In the **file list**, right-click the **Agave Picture** file, and then click **Rename**. Type **Agave Cactus** and then press Enter.

11 In the **file list**, right-click the **Garden Picture** file, and then click **Delete**. The **Delete File** message box displays, as shown in Figure 1.47.

Figure 1.47

Delete File message box asks for confirmation of delete

Another Way

In the Navigation pane, click your flash drive or other storage location name.

12 In the **Delete File** message box, click **Yes** to send the file to the Recycle Bin.

13 In the upper left corner of the window, click the **Back** button to move back to your main storage area.

14 In the **file list**, right-click the **XML Files** folder, and then click **Delete**. In the displayed **Delete Folder** message box, click **Yes**.

When you delete a folder, all files in the folder are also deleted.

Activity 1.15 | Compressing Files

Some files may be too large to send quickly as an e-mail attachment. For example, files containing graphics tend to be quite large. Windows 7 includes a feature with which you can *compress*—reduce the file size of—one or more files into a single file that uses a *.zip* file extension. These files can then be uncompressed for editing on any other computer running Windows 7. Many file types—such as most Microsoft Office 2007 files, Adobe Acrobat files, and JPEG picture files—do not benefit much from file compression. However, compression is often used to combine many files into one file for easy distribution.

1 With your storage device selected, and four folders and 16 files displayed in the **file list**, click the **Ration Coupons-1** file, hold down [Shift], and then click the second **Regulations** file. If your files are in a different order, select all 16 files, but not the folders. Notice that the Details pane indicates that 16 files are selected. If the total size of the files does not display, under *16 items selected*, click *Show more details*. Notice that the 16 files have a total size of 5.00 MB.

2 In the **file list**, right-click any of the selected files, and then from the displayed shortcut menu, point to **Send to**. Compare your screen with Figure 1.48.

Figure 1.48

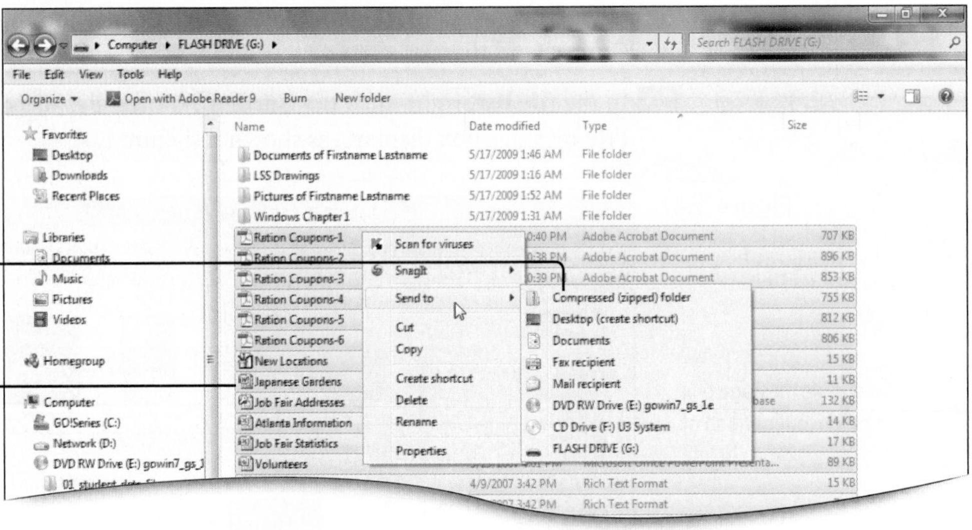

Compressed (zipped) folder command

Selected files

3 From the displayed list, click **Compressed (zipped)** folder, and then wait a moment for the files to be compressed.

The compressed folder displays the name of the file you right-clicked, but displays in edit mode so you can change the file name.

Note | To Work with Third-Party Zip Programs

If you are using a third-party zip program, such as WinZip™ or PKZIP™, you will need to use that program to complete this task—the procedure listed below will not work.

---

4 With the compressed folder name still in edit mode, type **Files of Firstname Lastname** and then press Enter. Notice that the compressed folder size is approximately 4.9 MB, which is not a great space savings. Compare your screen with Figure 1.49.

Figure 1.49

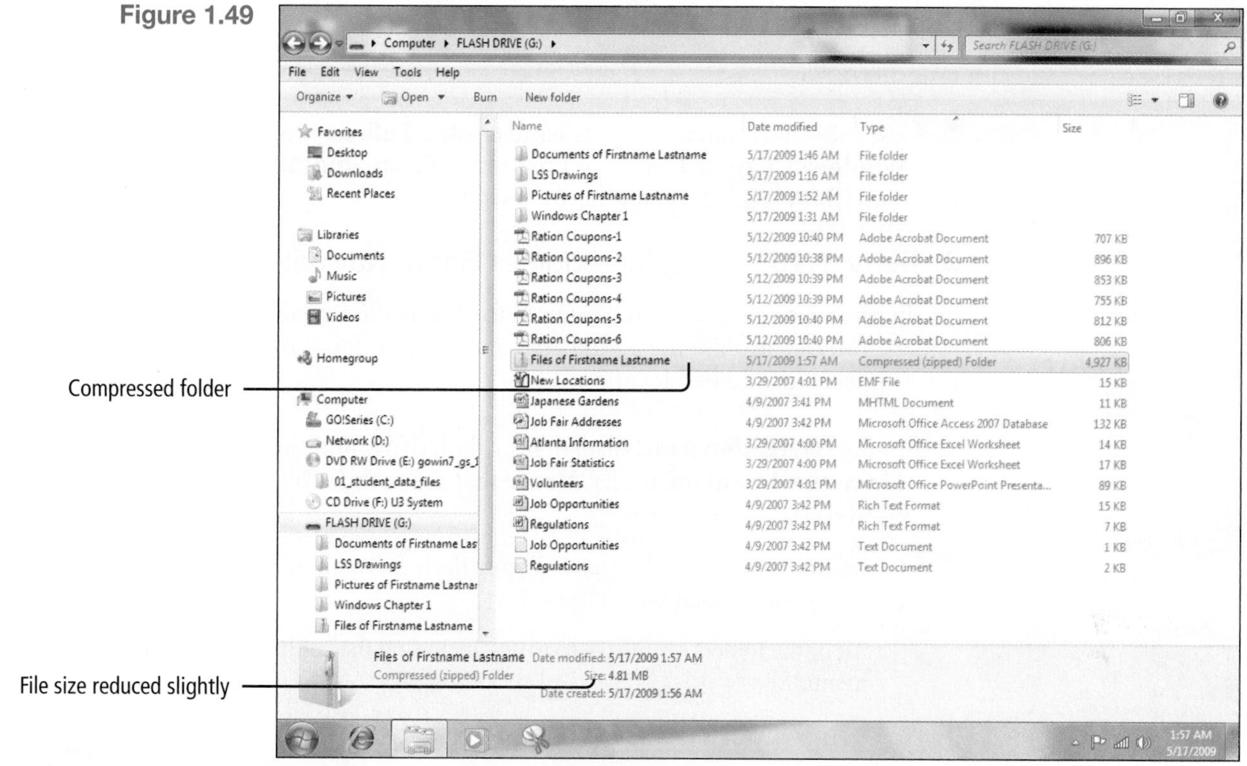

Compressed folder

File size reduced slightly

5 In the **file list**, double-click the **Files of Firstname Lastname** compressed folder. Compare your screen with Figure 1.50.

The files in the compressed folder are listed, along with their original sizes and their compressed sizes. The percent of space saved is indicated for each file. Some of the files show very little space savings, while in others the space saved is considerable. To extract the files from the compressed folder, you would click the *Extract all files* button on the Command bar. You can also open the files directly from the compressed folder.

Figure 1.50

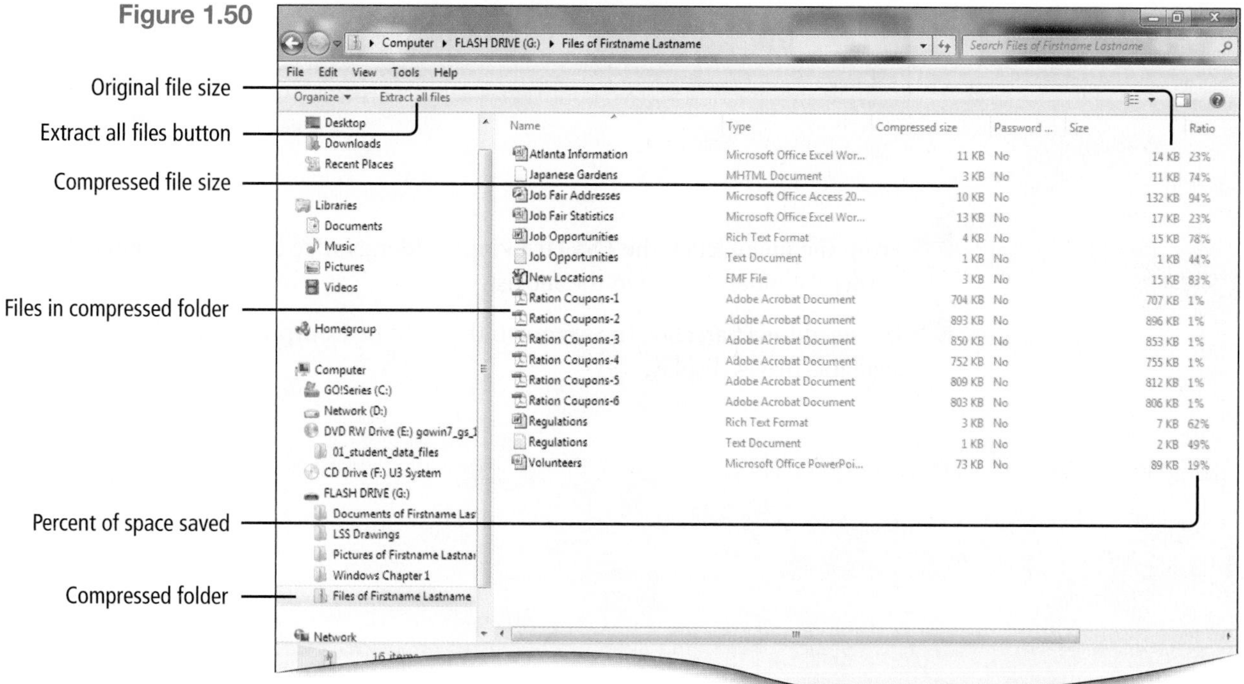

Original file size

Extract all files button

Compressed file size

Files in compressed folder

Percent of space saved

Compressed folder

> **More Knowledge** | Adding More Items to a Compressed Folder
>
> You can add more files to an existing compressed folder by dragging files and dropping them on the compressed folder. You can drag the files to the folder from anywhere, and you can also drag folders into a compressed folder.

6 Use the skills you practiced earlier to create a **Full-screen Snip**. **Save Snip** 🖫 to your **Windows Chapter 1** folder as **Lastname_Firstname_1B_Compressed_Folder** and then **Close** ⊠ the Snipping Tool window.

Activity 1.16 | Using the Address Bar to Navigate Drives and Folders

In previous activities, you have used the Navigation pane to move between drives and folders. You can also use the address bar at the top of the Windows Explorer window to move quickly to a desired location.

1 In the **Navigation** pane, display your flash drive, and then click the **Pictures of Firstname Lastname** folder. Notice that the path to the current folder displays in the address bar.

2 In the Address bar, to the right of your flash drive name, click the **arrow**, and then compare your screen with Figure 1.51.

All of the folders on the flash drive—including the compressed folder—display in a menu.

Figure 1.51

Flash drive arrow

Folders in flash drive, including compressed folder

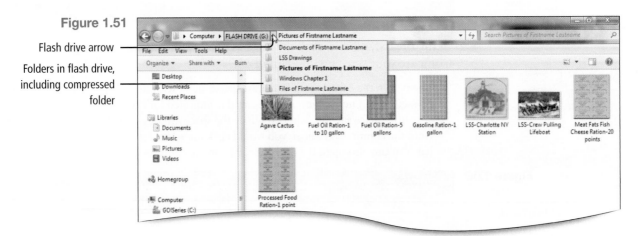

3 From the menu, click the **LSS Drawings** folder. Notice that the contents of the *LSS Drawings* folder display in the file list.

4 In the address bar, click the **arrow** to the right of **Computer**. Notice that all of the available drives display.

5 To the left of **Computer**, click the **arrow**, and then compare your screen with Figure 1.52.

The top-level items in the Navigation pane display in a menu, along with commands for the Control Panel and the Recycle Bin.

Figure 1.52

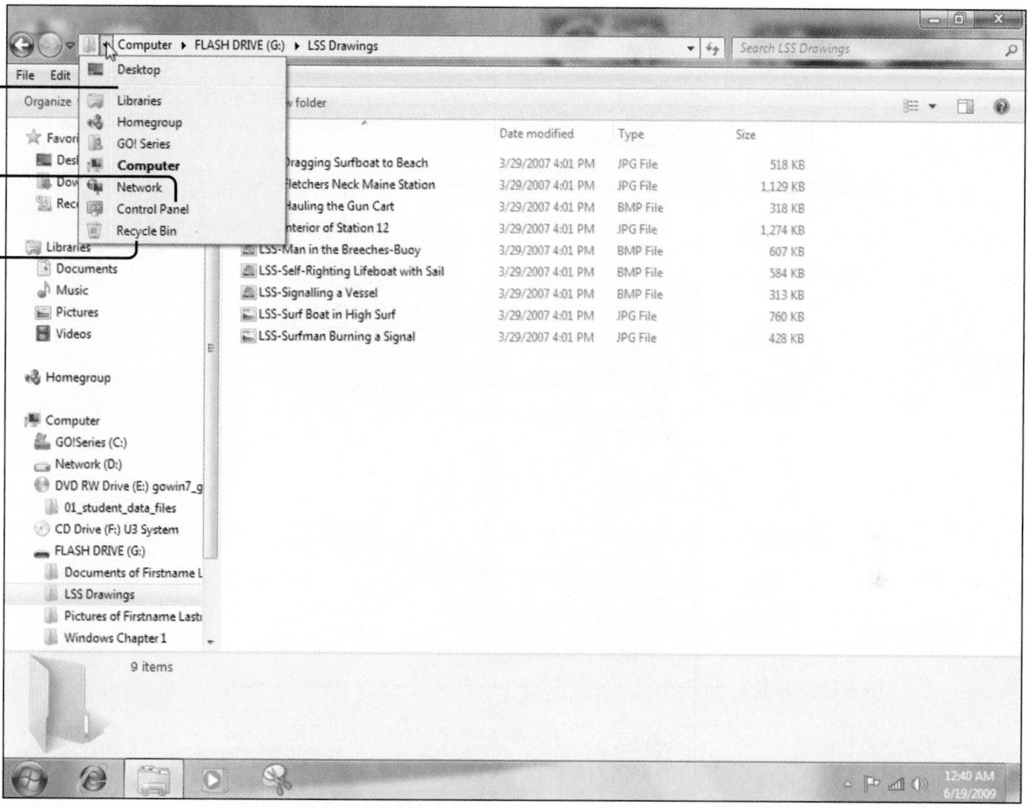

Top-level items in Navigation pane

Opens the Control Panel

Opens the Recycle Bin

6 Click anywhere in the **file list** to close the menu.

Objective 6 | Find Files and Folders

As you use a computer, you will likely accumulate a large number of files and folders. It's easy to forget where you stored a file, or what you named it. Windows 7 provides several search functions with which you can find files and folders. You can also add tags to files. *Tags* are custom file properties that help you find and organize your files. Tags are part of a file's *metadata*—items that record and display information about a file, such as a title, a rating, the file name, and the file size.

Activity 1.17 | Adding Descriptions and Tags to Files

1 Be sure your storage device is selected, with the contents of the **LSS Drawings** folder displayed in the file list. Also be sure the **Details** pane is open at the bottom of the window.

2 Click the first file in the **file list—LSS-Dragging Surfboat to Beach**. Move the pointer to the line at the top of the **Details** pane to display the [↕] pointer, and then drag the top of the Details pane to display three lines of details.

3 In the **Details** pane, click in the **Tags** box—to the right of the word *Tags*. Type **LSS** and then press ⟶. Type **LSS Boat** and then press ⟶. Type **Surfboat** and then compare your screen with Figure 1.53. Notice on the left side of the Details pane that the file type for this file is JPG—one of a number of image file types.

> When you add a tag, a semicolon immediately displays to the right of the insertion point. Semicolons separate multiple tags.

Figure 1.53

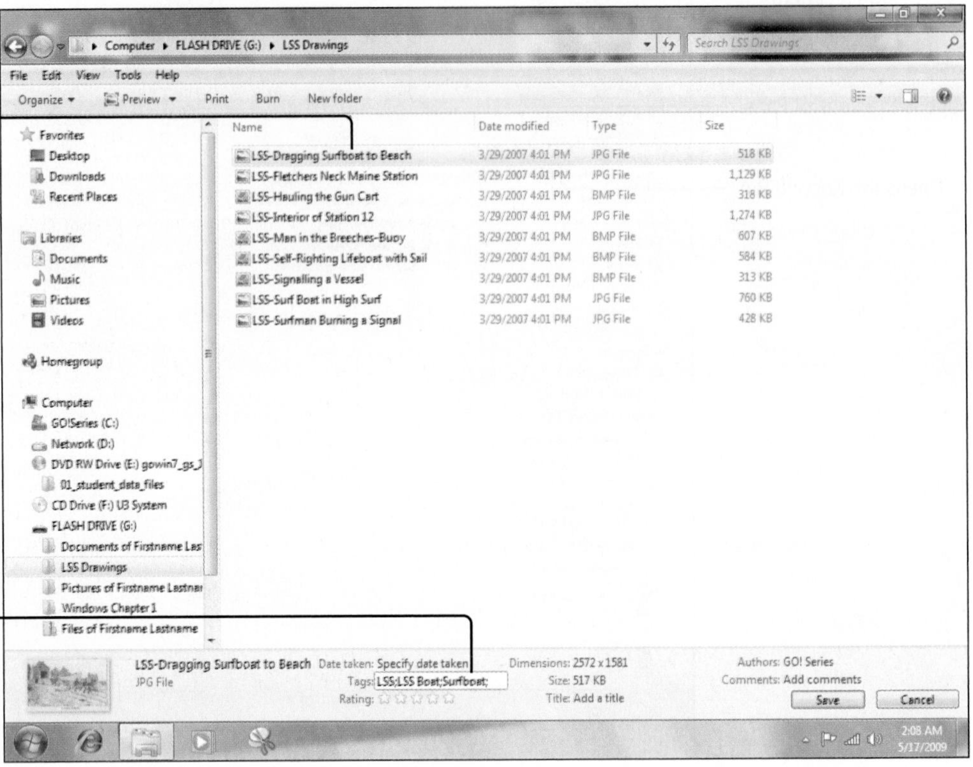

Selected file ——————

New tags added ——————

4 Press ⟨Enter⟩ to confirm the tags. Using the procedure you just practiced, add the same three tags to the **LSS-Surf Boat in High Surf** file. Notice on the left side of the Details pane that the file type for this file is JPG or JPEG.

5 Click the **LSS-Self-Righting Lifeboat with Sail** file. Notice that there is no place to add a tag.

> This image is a bitmap image, which does not support tags. Most Microsoft Office 2007 and 2010 default file formats support tags, as do many other file formats.

6 In the **Navigation** pane, click the **Pictures of Firstname Lastname** folder, and then click the file **LSS-Charlotte NY Station**. Add the following tags: **LSS** and **LSS Boat** and **LSS Boat Ramp** and then press ⟨Enter⟩.

7 In the **Details** pane, click the **Title** box, type **Life Saving Station at Charlotte, NY** and then press ⟨Enter⟩.

8 In the **file list**, right-click the **LSS-Charlotte NY Station** file, and then from the shortcut menu, click **Properties**. In the **Properties** dialog box, click the **Details tab**.

> The items you entered in the Details pane display, and there are several other categories of tags that you can add, including a rating of the picture or document.

9 In the **Properties** dialog box, under **Description**, click the fourth **Rating** star from the left. Under **Origin**, click the **Copyright** box, type **Public Domain** and then compare your screen with Figure 1.54.

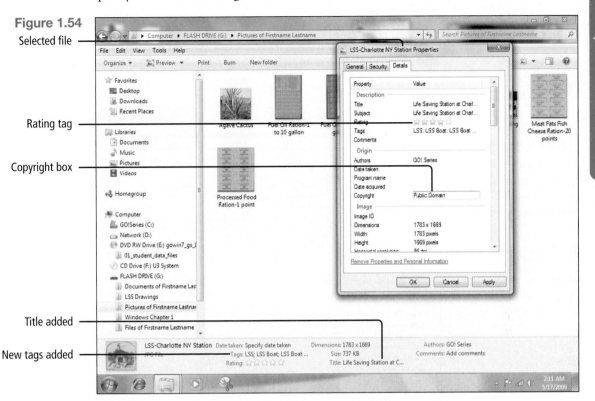

Figure 1.54

Selected file

Rating tag

Copyright box

Title added

New tags added

10 At the bottom of the **Properties** dialog box, click **OK**.

Activity 1.18 | Finding Files and Folders and Creating a Search Folder

1 In the **Navigation** pane, click your storage location name. Be sure your storage device is selected, and four folders, one compressed folder, and 16 files display in the file list.

2 Near the upper right corner of the window, click in the **Search** box, type **J** and then in the **file list**, examine the results of your search, as shown in Figure 1.55. If your search results do not display in the list format, to the right of the *Change your view* button [icon], click the *More options* arrow, and then click Details.

The program found all files and folders with words that begin with the letter *J*, along with all file types (file extensions) with words that begin with the letter *J*—in this case, all JPEG image files. Your files may display in a different order.

Figure 1.55

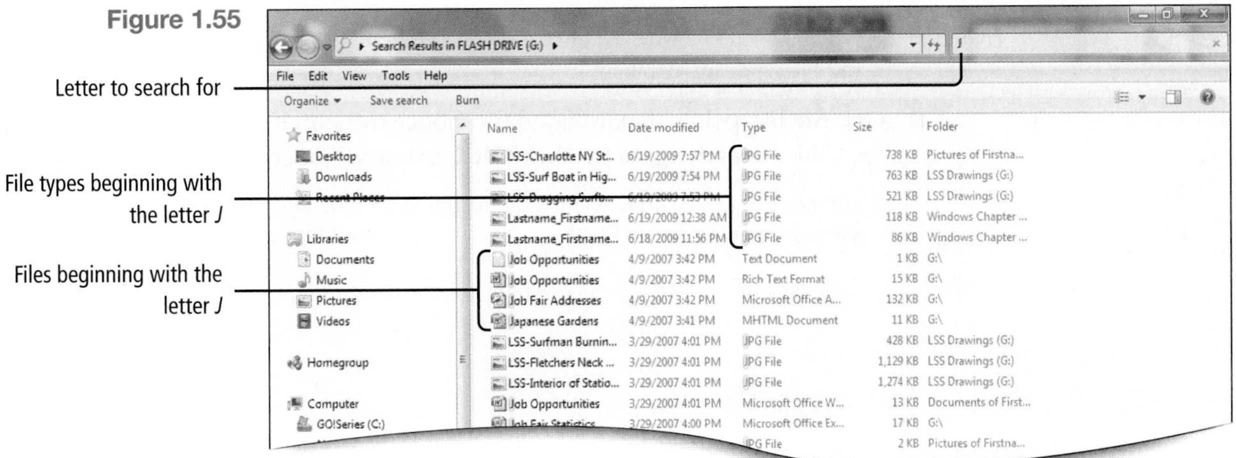

Letter to search for

File types beginning with the letter *J*

Files beginning with the letter *J*

3 With the letter *J* already in the **Search** box, type the letter **P** and examine the search results. Notice that the only files, folders, or file types in your storage device that begin with the letters *JP* are the JPEG image files.

4 Press [Bksp], and notice that the search results again display all files, folders, and file types that contain the letter *J*.

5 Now type **ob** to complete the word *Job*. Notice that five files display, as shown in Figure 1.56.

Figure 1.56

Search term ——

Files that begin with *Job* ——

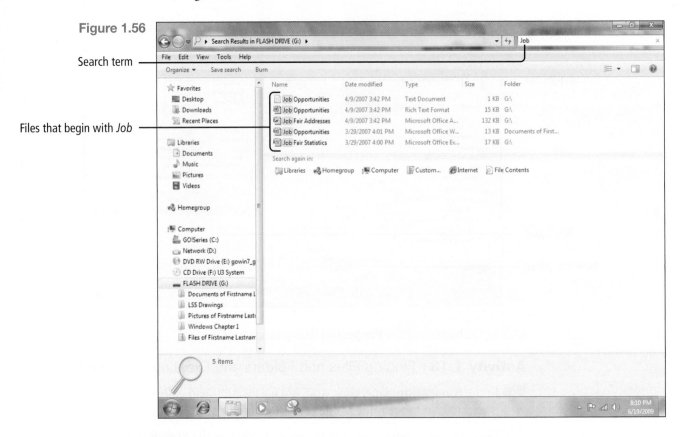

6 Press [Bksp] three times, type **LSS** and then notice that files and folders from various locations display in the file list.

7 Press [Spacebar], type **boat** and then notice that only one file or folder meets this search condition, even though you added *LSS Boat* as a tag to several files. Also notice that the file that was found had both search words, but they do not have to be next to each other.

> When you enter a word or phrase in the Search pane, only the file names, folder names, and file types are searched.

8 In the **file list**, below the displayed file, notice the search alternatives that are available. Under **Search again in**, click **File Contents**. Notice that three files display.

> The *File Contents* search extends the search to include tags, text that is a portion of a file name, or text inside the file.

9 On the Command bar, click the **Save search** button. In the displayed **Save As** dialog box, click **Save**. Compare your screen with Figure 1.57.

A *search folder* is saved on your computer under **Favorites**—not on your removable storage device. A search folder retains all of the search conditions you specified during your search, and recreates the search every time you click the search folder. As you add more pictures with the *LSS Boat* tag to your removable storage device, the search folder will find them. It is important to remember that the search folder will only search the location you specified—it will not search the rest of the computer.

Figure 1.57

New search folder ————

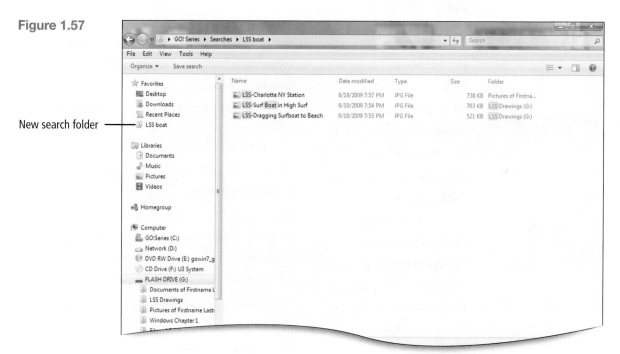

10 Use the skills you practiced earlier to create a **Full-screen Snip**. Save the snip to your **Windows Chapter 1** folder as **Lastname_Firstname_1B_Search_Folder** and submit all three file snips from Project 1B as directed. If you are directed to print the files, use the skills practiced in Activity 1.9 to create a WordPad document, add your name, drag the three snip files from this project, and then print the document. It is not necessary to save the WordPad file once you have printed it.

11 In the title bar, click the **Close** button to close the Windows Explorer window. Select and **Delete** the files and shortcuts you saved on the desktop, and then **Close** the gadgets that you added to the desktop.

More Knowledge | Using Wildcards in Searches

When you are searching for a particular type of file, you can specify the extension by using a wildcard, followed by the extension. A *wildcard* takes the place of one or more characters in a search. For example, if you wanted to search for all of your Excel 2007 files in the My Documents folder, select the folder, and then type *.xlsx in the Search box. All files with the *.xlsx* extension will display. If you want to display all of your Excel files, including older versions (with the *.xls* extension), type *.xls. This search will locate all *.xls* and *.xlsx* files. Similarly, you can search for all files beginning with *Fun* by typing *Fun**, which will return all files with those first three letters, including *Fundamentals of Business* and *Fun with Trombones*.

End **You have completed Project 1B**

Content-Based Assessments

Summary

Windows 7 is a robust operating system that enables you to easily locate information and programs. It enables you to create, rename, move, copy, and delete files and folders. You can add key words and other information to the files to make searching easier and more accurate.

Key Terms

Active window 16	Folder 29	ScreenTip 6
Address bar 6	Gadget................................11	Scroll box 26
Aero...................................8	Gadget controls 12	Search box 6
All Programs 14	Graphical user interface (GUI)................................7	Search folder 47
Archive 35		Shake................................21
Ascending order.............32	Hard drive 7	Shortcut menu 6
CD 31	Hardware 3	Snip 18
Click 5	Horizontal scroll bar 22	Snipping Tool 18
Clipboard 35	Icon 4	Start button 4
Close button.....................6	Jump list 23	Start menu 13
Command bar 4	Libraries 5	Status area 4
Compress 40	Library pane 6	Submenu...........................14
Computer icon 4	Local disk 29	System tray.......................4
Context-sensitive command 6	Maximize 19	Tags 43
	Menu 6	Taskbar 4
Descending order.............32	Menu bar............................6	Thumb drive 31
Desktop..............................3	Metadata...........................43	Thumbnail 22
Desktop background 10	Minimize 19	Title bar..............................6
Details pane 6	Mouse pointer 4	Toolbar 6
Dialog box.........................9	Navigation pane 6	USB drive 31
Double-click 6	Notification area................4	Vertical scroll bar 22
Drag................................25	Operating system.............3	Wildcard 47
Drive 7	Paint 22	Window 5
DVD 31	Peek..................................21	Window name.................15
Edit mode 31	Pinned programs area 14	Windows 3
Favorites...........................6	Pointer................................4	Windows Aero 8
File.....................................29	Recycle Bin.......................4	Windows Explorer 5
File extension 37	Restore 19	WordPad 16
File list..............................7	Right-click 6	
Flash drive.......................31	Screen saver.....................8	

Content-Based Assessments

Screen ID

Identify each element of the screen by matching callout numbers shown in Figure 1.58 to a corresponding description.

Figure 1.58

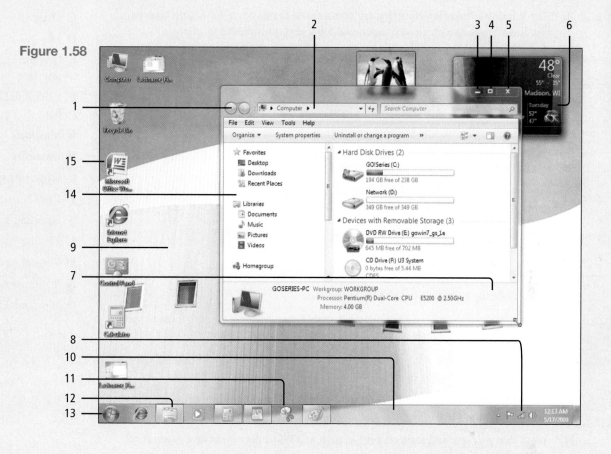

_____ A. Address bar

_____ B. Back button

_____ C. Close button

_____ D. Desktop

_____ E. Details pane

_____ F. Gadget

_____ G. Icon

_____ H. Maximize button

_____ I. Minimize button

_____ J. Navigation pane

_____ K. Notification area

_____ L. Snipping Tool button

_____ M. Start button

_____ N. Taskbar

_____ O. Windows Explorer button

Matching

Match each term in the second column with its correct definition in the first column. Write the letter of the term on the blank line in front of the correct definition.

_____ 1. The Windows 7 user interface that features a three-dimensional look, with transparent window frames, live previews of open windows, and multiple color schemes.

_____ 2. A program that captures a screen or part of a screen.

_____ 3. Displays information about the drive, folder, or file selected in the file list.

_____ 4. A set of instructions that coordinates the activities of your computer.

_____ 5. A computer interface that shows documents as they will look in their final form and uses icons to represent programs.

_____ 6. A simple drawing program included with Windows 7.

_____ 7. Displays the Start button and the name of any open documents; it may also display shortcut buttons for other programs.

_____ 8. Command at the bottom of the Start menu that takes you to all available programs on your computer.

_____ 9. To remove the window from the screen without closing it.

_____ 10. To increase the size of a window to fill the screen.

_____ 11. The bar at the right side of a window that enables you to move up and down to view information that extends beyond the top and bottom of the screen.

_____ 12. The bar at the bottom of a window that enables you to move left and right to view information that extends beyond the left and right edges of the screen.

_____ 13. Move the mouse pointer while holding down the left mouse button, and then release at the appropriate time.

_____ 14. Work that you save and store on a drive, such as a Word document or a PowerPoint presentation.

_____ 15. A program that enables you to create and manage folders, and copy, move, sort, and delete files.

A All Programs

B Details pane

C Drag

D File

E Graphical user interface

F Horizontal scroll bar

G Maximize

H Minimize

I Operating system

J Paint

K Snipping Tool

L Taskbar

M Vertical scroll bar

N Windows Aero

O Windows Explorer

Multiple Choice

Circle the correct answer.

1. In the Windows Explorer window, this pane displays Favorites, Libraries, Computer, and Network information.
   - **a.** Preview
   - **b.** Navigation
   - **c.** Details

2. The working area of the Windows 7 screen—consisting of program icons, a taskbar, a Start button, and gadgets—is the:
   - **a.** desktop
   - **b.** window
   - **c.** Notification area

3. The arrow, I-beam, or other symbol that shows the location or position of the mouse on your screen is the mouse:
   - **a.** button
   - **b.** cursor
   - **c.** pointer

4. The area on the right side of the taskbar that keeps you informed about processes that are occurring in the background, such as antivirus software, network connections, and other utility programs, is the:
   - **a.** Quick Launch toolbar
   - **b.** Notification area
   - **c.** program icon

5. Custom file properties such as names, places, and descriptions that are added to files are called:
   - **a.** jump lists
   - **b.** details
   - **c.** metadata

6. You can activate this by pointing to an object and clicking the right mouse button.
   - **a.** active window
   - **b.** shortcut menu
   - **c.** gadget

7. When you create a new folder, the folder name displays:
   - **a.** in edit mode
   - **b.** in the Details pane
   - **c.** on the desktop

8. When you create a search folder, it displays in the Navigation pane under this category:
   - **a.** Favorites
   - **b.** Computer
   - **c.** Libraries

9. A dynamic program—such as a clock, a stock market ticker, or a weather window—that displays on the desktop is a:
   - **a.** gadget
   - **b.** tag
   - **c.** snip

10. The three or four characters to the right of the period in a file name is called:
    - **a.** metadata
    - **b.** a wildcard
    - **c.** a file extension

Skills Review | Project **1C** Using Windows 7

Apply a combination of the 1A and 1B skills.

In the following Skills Review, you will copy files from your student data disk to a flash drive, create and rename folders, and move files. You will also add tags to files and search for files using the Search box. Your completed documents will look similar to the ones shown in Figure 1.59.

Project Files

For Project 1C, you will need the following files:

36 sample files, and two folders containing 14 additional files

You will save your documents as:

Lastname_Firstname_1C_Screen_Saver
Lastname_Firstname_1C_Desktop
Lastname_Firstname_1C_Folders
Lastname_Firstname_1C_Tags

Project Results

Figure 1.59

(Project 1C Using Windows 7 continues on the next page)

Content-Based Assessments

Skills Review | Project 1C Using Windows 7 (continued)

1 Turn on your computer and if necessary follow the log-on instructions required for the computer you are using.

2 Move the pointer to an open area of the desktop, and then right-click. From the shortcut menu, move the pointer to the bottom of the list, and then click **Personalize**. At the bottom of the **Personalization** window, click the **Screen Saver** button. Click the **Screen saver box arrow**, and then from the displayed list, click **Bubbles**.

3 If the **Snipping Tool** does not display on your taskbar, click the **Start** button, point to **All Programs**, click **Accessories**, right-click **Snipping Tool**, and then click **Pin to Taskbar**. On the taskbar, click the **Snipping Tool** button. In the **Snipping Tool** window, click the arrow to the right of the **New** button, and then click **Full-screen Snip**.

4 In the **Snipping Tool** window, click the **Save Snip** button. In the **Save As** dialog box, in the left pane, scroll down to display the **Computer** drives. Click your flash drive, and then in the Command bar, click the **New folder** button. Name the new folder **Windows Project C** Press [Enter], and then press [Enter] again to open the new folder. In the **File name** box, type **Lastname_Firstname_1C_ Screen_Saver** Be sure the **Save as type** box displays *JPEG file*. Click **Save**, and then **Close** the Snipping Tool window.

5 If you want to use the Bubbles screen saver, at the bottom of the Screen Saver Settings dialog box, click OK; otherwise, click Cancel.

6 At the bottom of the **Personalization** window, click **Desktop Background**. Use the vertical scroll bar to display the **United States** desktop backgrounds, and then click the picture of the **stone arch**. Click **Save changes** to apply the new background, and then **Close** the Personalization window.

7 Click the **Start** button, point to **All Programs**, and then click **Accessories**. Right-click **WordPad**, point to **Send to**, click **Desktop (create shortcut)**, and then click in any open area of the desktop.

8 In an open area of the desktop, right-click to display a shortcut menu, and then click **Gadgets**. Double-click the **Clock** gadget, double-click the **Stocks** gadget, and then double-click the **CPU Meter** gadget. **Close** the Gadgets window. Point to the **CPU Usage** gadget, and then click the **Larger size** button. Drag the **CPU Usage** gadget to the top of the desktop.

9 Use the skills you practiced to create a **Full-screen Snip** of the desktop, **Save** it in the **Windows Project C** folder as **Lastname_Firstname_1C_Desktop** and then **Close** the Snipping Tool window.

10 On the taskbar, click the **Windows Explorer** button. If this button is not available, click the Start button, point to All Programs, click Accessories, and then click Windows Explorer. Insert your student data CD. In the **Windows Explorer** window, in the **Navigation** pane, click the drive that contains your student data files. To the left of the drive name, click the open arrow to display the **01_student_data_files** folder, and then click that folder to display the folders and files in the file list.

11 In the **Navigation** pane, in the drive that contains your student files, be sure the folders display. In the **file list**, drag the **XML Files** folder to the **Windows Project C** folder on your flash drive.

12 At the top of the **file list**, click the **Type** column heading. Widen the **Type** column so you can see all of the file types. Click the first **Adobe Acrobat** document—*Ration Coupons-1*—, hold down [Shift], and then click the last **Adobe Acrobat** document—*Ration Coupons-6*. Drag the selected files to the **Windows Project C** folder on your flash drive. Then, select all of the files with a **Type** that begins *Microsoft Office*. Drag these 15 files to the **Windows Project C** folder on your flash drive.

13 In the **Navigation** pane, locate your flash drive, and then click the **Windows Project C** folder. On the Command bar click the **New Folder** button, and then name the folder **Adobe Acrobat Files** Select the six **Adobe Acrobat Files** and drag them to the folder you just created. In the **Navigation** pane, expand the **Windows Project C** folder, and then click the **Windows Project C** folder to display the folder contents.

14 In the **file list**, right-click the file **Volunteers**, and then click **Rename**. Rename the file **Job Fair Volunteers** In the same list of files, right-click the **Lightning** file, and then from the shortcut menu, click **Delete**. In the message box, click **Yes**.

15 At the top of the **file list**, click the **Name** column heading as necessary to display the folders and files in ascending (*a* to *z*) order. Use the skills you practiced to create a **Full-screen Snip** of the Windows Explorer window, **Save** it in the **Windows Project C** folder as

(Project 1C Using Windows 7 continues on the next page)

Skills Review | Project 1C Using Windows 7 (continued)

Lastname_Firstname_1C_Folders and then **Close** the Snipping Tool window.

16 In the **file list**, click the **Job Fair Statistics** file. In the **Details** pane, click to the right of **Tags**. In the **Tags** box, type **Atlanta** press →, and then type **Job Fair** Add the same tags to the **Atlanta Information** file.

17 In the **Search** box, type **Atlanta** and then press Enter. In the **file list**, click **File Contents** to include files with the word *Atlanta* in the files or in the file tags. If necessary, change the display to Details. Use the skills you practiced to create a **Full-screen Snip** of the Windows Explorer window, **Save** it in the **Windows Project C**

folder as **Lastname_Firstname_1C_Tags** and then **Close** the Snipping Tool window.

18 Submit all four snips as directed. If you are directed to print the files, use the skills practiced in Activity 1.9 to create a WordPad document, add your name, drag the four snip files from this project, and then print the document. It is not necessary to save the WordPad file once you have printed it.

19 Remove all desktop and taskbar shortcuts that you created in this project, and then **Close** all three gadgets that you added.

End **You have completed Project 1C** ——————————

Glossary

Active window The window in which the mouse pointer's movements commands, or text entry occur when two or more windows are open.

Address bar A toolbar that displays the organizational path to the active file, folder, or window.

Aero See Windows Aero.

All Programs Command at the bottom of the Start menu that takes you to all available programs on your computer.

Archive To back up files and store them somewhere other than the main hard drive.

Ascending order Files or folders listed from *a* to *z* when sorted.

Background See Desktop background.

CD A compact disc—an optical storage device used to store data and which can be read-only or read-write.

Click To press the left mouse button one time.

Clipboard A temporary storage area in Windows that stores the most recently copied item.

Close button A shortcut button in a title bar that closes a window or a program.

Command bar The area at the top of a window that displays commands relevant to the open window.

Compress Reduce the size of a file or combine several files into one.

Computer icon An icon that represents the computer on which you are working, and that provides access to the drives, folders, and files on your computer.

Content pane Displays files and folders stored in the selected disk drive or folder in the Navigation pane.

Context-sensitive command A command associated with activities in which you are engaged; often activated by right-clicking a screen item.

Descending order Files or folders listed from *z* to *a* when sorted.

Desktop The working area of the Windows 7 screen, consisting of program icons, a taskbar, a sidebar, and a Start button.

Desktop background The picture, pattern, or color that displays on the desktop.

Details pane Displays details about the drive, folder, or file selected in the Content pane.

Dialog box A box that asks you to make a decision about an individual object or topic. Dialog boxes do not have Minimize buttons.

Double-click Press the left mouse button two times in rapid succession, using caution not to move the mouse.

Drag Move the mouse pointer while holding down the left mouse button, and then release at the appropriate time.

Drive An area of storage that is formatted with the Windows file system and that has a drive letter such as C.

DVD A digital video (or versatile) disc—an optical storage device used to store data, and which can be read-only or read-write.

Edit mode A Windows mode that enables you to change the name of a file or folder, and works the same in all Windows applications.

Favorites The top part of the Navigation pane that displays favorite destinations associated with the current user.

File Work that you save and store on a drive, such as a Word document or a PowerPoint presentation.

File extension The three or four characters to the right of the period in a file name. Extensions tell the computer the program to use to open the file. File extensions can be displayed or hidden.

File list Displays the contents of the current folder or library.

Flash drive A small storage device that plugs into a computer USB port; also called a thumb drive or a USB drive.

Folder Storage area, represented on the screen by a picture of a paper file folder, used to store files or other folders.

Gadget A dynamic program—such as a clock, a stock market ticker, or a weather window—that displays on the desktop, usually in the Windows Sidebar.

Gadget controls A set of tools that includes a Drag gadget button in the shape of 12 small dots, an Options button in the shape of a wrench, a Larger/Smaller size button, and a Close button.

Graphical user interface (GUI) A computer interface that shows documents as they will look in their final form and uses icons to represent programs.

Hard drive A large disk drive inside your computer, also referred to as a Local Disk.

Hardware The computer memory, disk drive space, attached devices such as printers and scanners, and the central processing unit (CPU).

Horizontal scroll bar The bar at the bottom of a window that enables you to move left and right to view information that extends beyond the left and right edges of the screen.

Icon A graphic representation; often a small image on a button that enables you to run a program or program function.

Jump list A shortcut menu from an icon on the taskbar that displays frequent destinations you might want to visit from that program.

Libraries Folders used to sort files by file type.

Library pane Displays above the file list when a library is selected in the Navigation pane.

Local disk A large disk drive inside your computer, also referred to as a hard disk.

Maximize To increase the size of a window to fill the screen.

Menu A list of commands within a category.

Menu bar The bar near the top of a window that lists the names of menu categories.

Metadata Information about a file, such as tags, a title, a rating, the file name, and the file size.

Minimize To remove the window from the screen without closing it. Minimized windows can be reopened by clicking the associated button in the taskbar.

Mouse pointer The arrow, I-beam, or other symbol that shows the location or position of the mouse on your screen. Also called the pointer.

Navigation pane The pane on the left side of the Computer or Windows Explorer window that contains Favorites, Libraries, access to personal files and folders, and other items.

Notification area Area on the right side of the taskbar that keeps you informed about processes that are occurring in the background, such as antivirus software, network connections, and other utility programs. It also displays the time.

Operating system A set of instructions that coordinates the activities of your computer. Microsoft Windows 7 is an operating system.

Paint A program included with Windows in which graphics are created or edited.

Peek Use the *Show desktop* button to make the open windows transparent so you can see the desktop.

Pinned programs area An area at the top of the Start menu that is reserved for programs that you want to display permanently, although you can also delete programs from this area.

Pointer See mouse pointer.

Recycle Bin A storage area for files that have been deleted. Files can be recovered from the Recycle bin or permanently removed.

Restore Return a window to the size it was before it was maximized, using the Restore Down button.

Right-click Click the right mouse button to activate a shortcut menu.

Screen saver A picture or animation that displays on your screen after a set period of computer inactivity.

ScreenTip A small box, activated by holding the pointer over a button or other screen object, that displays the name of a screen element.

Scroll box The box in the vertical and horizontal scroll bars that can be dragged to reposition the document on the screen. The size of the scroll box also indicates the relative size of the document.

Search box A box in which you type a search word or phrase.

Search folder Retains all of the search conditions you specified during your search, and recreates the search every time you click the search folder.

Shake Use the title bar to move a window back and forth quickly to hide all other open windows.

Shortcut menu A menu activated by placing the pointer over an object and clicking the right mouse button.

Snip A screen or part of a screen captured using the Snipping Tool.

Snipping tool A program used to capture a screen or part of a screen.

Start button The button on the left side of the taskbar that is used to start programs, change system settings, find Windows help, or shut down the computer.

Start menu A menu that enables you to access the programs on your computer, and also enables you to change the way Windows operates, to access and configure your network, and to get help and support when it is needed.

Status area Another name for the notification area on the right side of the taskbar.

Submenu A second-level menu activated by selecting a menu option.

System tray Another name for the notification area on the right side of the taskbar.

Tags Custom file properties such as names, places, and descriptions that are added to files to enable you to categorize and find files more quickly.

Taskbar Displays the Start button and the name of any open documents. The taskbar also displays shortcut buttons for other programs.

Thumb drive A small storage device that plugs into a computer USB port; also called a USB drive or a flash drive.

Thumbnail A miniature representation of the contents of a window or file.

Title bar Displays the program icon, the name of the document, and the name of the program. The Minimize, Maximize/Restore Down, and Close buttons are grouped on the right side of the title bar.

USB drive A small storage device that plugs into a computer USB port; also called a thumb drive or a flash drive.

Vertical scroll bar The bar at the right side of a window that enables you to move up and down to view information that extends beyond the top and bottom of the screen.

Wildcard A character, such as an asterisk, that can be used to match any number of characters in a file search.

Window A box that displays information or a program, such as a letter, Excel, or a calculator. Windows usually consist of title bars, toolbars, menu bars, and status bars. A window will always have a Minimize button.

Window name The name that displays in a window's title bar.

Windows An operating system that coordinates the activities of a computer.

Windows Aero The Windows user interface that features a three-dimensional look, with transparent window frames, live previews of open windows, and multiple color schemes. Aero is an acronym for **A**uthentic, **E**nergetic, **R**eflective, **O**pen.

Windows Explorer A program that enables you to create and manage folders, and manage copy, move, sort, and delete files.

WordPad A simple word processing program that comes with Windows 7.

Index

A

Accessories programs, 15–20. *See also* **Calculator; Paint; Snipping Tool**
active window, 16
address bar, 5–6
Aero interface, 8, 21–23
Alerts!
    file type difference, 38
    gadgets, 11
    hidden taskbar, 14
    icon differences, 4
    screen differences, 3
    window variances (Windows Explorer window), 5, 8
All Programs command, 14–15
Alt key and Tab key, 23
Architecture backgrounds, 10
Auto Play dialog box, 30
auto-hide feature (for taskbar), 14

B

Back command, 15
backgrounds, desktop, 10
BMP files, 38
Budget file, 38

C

Calculator, 15
CD (Compact Disc), 31
click (right-click, double-click), 6
Close button
    for gadgets, 12
    for windows, 5–6
closing windows, 27
columns, in file list, 33
Command bar, 4
Compact Disc (CD), 31
compressing files, 40–42
Computer icon, 6
context-sensitive commands, 6
Control Panel, 9, 43
copying files, 35–37
customizing
    desktop, 8–10
    taskbar, 22–24

D

deleting. *See also* **removing**
    files, 37–40
    Recycle Bin, 4, 39, 43
Descriptions for files, 43–45
desktop, 3–10
    exploring, 3–8

    personalizing/customizing, 8–10
    shortcuts added to, 17–18
desktop backgrounds, 10
Desktop Icon Settings dialog box, 11
Details pane, 5–8, 29–30, 33, 37, 40, 43–44
diagonal resize pointer, 25
dialog boxes, 9. *See also specific dialog boxes*
Digital Video (or Versatile) Disc (DVD), 31
displaying windows, 20–21
Documents (library), 29
Documents of Firstname Lastname folder, 32, 38
double-click, 6
drag, 25
Drag gadget (gadget control), 12
drive letters, 7, 31
drives, 7. *See also* **hard drives**
DVD (Digital Video (or Versatile) Disc), 31

E

Excel, 20, 37, 47
Explorer. *See* **Internet Explorer icon; Windows Explorer**
external hard drive, 29
Extract all files button, 41

F

Favorites, 5–6
file extensions, 38
file list, 5–7, 33–35
file types, 38
files. *See also specific files*
    compressing, 40–42
    copying, 35–37
    descriptions for, 43–45
    finding, 45–47
    folders/files management (project 1B), 28–47
    moving/renaming/deleting, 37–40
    tags on, 43–45
finding folders/files, 45–47
flash drives (USB/thumb drives), 29–39, 42
folders. *See also specific folders*
    creating, 31–32
    finding, 45–47
    folders/files management (Project 1B), 28–47
    moving, 33–35
    renaming, 33–35
    search, 45–47
Full-screen Snip, 18, 24, 35, 42, 47

G

gadget controls, 12–13
gadgets, 4, 11–13
Gadgets dialog box, 11, 13

graphical user interface (GUI), 3. *See also* Aero interface
GUI. *See* graphical user interface

H

hard drives. *See also* flash drives
   defined, 7
   external, 29
   letter notation for, 7, 31
   local, 29, 31, 35
   removable, 7, 29–30, 32, 35, 47
hardware, 3
hiding
   taskbar, 14
   windows, 20–21
horizontal scroll bar, 22, 26

I

icons, 4. *See also* shortcuts
   computer, 6
   defined, 4
   on desktop, 17–18
   differences in, 4
Internet Explorer icon, 4
Invitation file, 37

J-K

JPEG/JPG files, 19, 24, 38, 40, 44–46
jump list, 23
key terms, 49

L

Larger size (gadget control), 12
libraries, 29
Library pane, 5–6
Life Saving Service Drawings folder, 34–35, 44
local disk, 29, 31, 35
LSS Boat tag, 46–47
LSS Drawings, 35, 42–43
LSS-Charlotte NY Station, 44
LSS-Dragging Surfboat to Beach, 43
LSS-Surf Boat in High Surf, 44

M

managing files/folders (Project 1B), 28–47
Maximize button, 19, 29
maximizing windows, 19–20
memory, 29
Menu bar, 5–6
menus, 6
metadata, 43. *See also* tags
Microsoft Office, 20, 37–38, 40, 44
minimizing windows, 19–20
mouse
   double-click, 6
   pointer, 4
   right-click, 6

moving. *See also* removing
   files, 37–40
   folders, 33–35
   windows, 24–27
multiple open windows, 20, 22
Music (library), 29

N

names, window, 15
navigating Windows Explorer, 29–31
Navigation pane, 5–6, 30
notification area, 4

O

open windows, multiple, 20, 22
operating systems, 3, 49. *See also* Windows 7
Options (gadget control), 12

P

Paint (program), 21–22
Personalization window, 8–10
Pictures (library), 29
pinned program area, 14
pinning shortcuts, to Start menu, 16–17
PKZIP, 40
Preview button, 9
Print dialog box, 27
Properties dialog box, 14, 24, 44–45

R

recently used programs, 14
Recycle Bin, 4, 39, 43
removable drives/storage devices, 7, 29–30, 32, 35, 47. *See also* flash drives
removing. *See also* deleting
   auto-hide feature, 14
   gadgets, 11–12
   pinned programs, 14
renaming
   files, 37–40
   folders, 33–35
resize pointer, diagonal, 25
resizing windows, 24–27
Restore Down button, 16, 19–20, 22
restoring windows, 19–20
Ribbons (screen saver), 9
right-click, 6

S

Save As dialog box, 18–19, 24, 27, 35, 47
screen
   differences in, 3
   elements, 4
   scroll box, 26
Screen Saver Settings dialog box, 9
screen savers, 8–9

screen shots (snips), 18. *See also* Snipping Tool
ScreenTip, 5–6, 34
scroll bars
    horizontal, 22, 26
    vertical, 22, 24–26, 37, 38
scroll box, 26
scrolling windows, 24–27
search box, 5–6
search folder, 45–47
Search programs and files box, 16
Send to command, 17–18
shortcut menus, 6
shortcuts
    desktop, 17–18
    Start menu, 16–17
    taskbar, 18–19
Show desktop button, 21, 24–25
Show more details command, 37
Show on Desktop, 6
Slide Show gadget, 13
Smaller size (gadget control), 12
Snipping Tool, 18–19, 24, 35, 42, 47
snips (screen shots), 18
Start button, 4
Start menu, 12–19
status area. *See* notification area
storage. *See also* flash drives; hard drives
    devices, 31
    drives, 7
    memory, 29
    removable devices, 7, 29–30, 32, 35, 47
    temporary, 29
submenus, 14
Survey Letter, 38
system tray. *See* notification area

T

Tab key, Alt key and, 23
tags, 43–47
taskbar, 4
    auto-hide feature for, 14
    customizing, 22–24
    defined, 4
temporary storage, 29
terms (key terms), 49
thumb drives. *See* flash drives
thumbnails, 22

title bar, 5–6
toolbar, 5–6

U

unhiding taskbar, 14
USB drives. *See* flash drives
USB (Universal Serial Bus) port, 31

V

vertical scroll bar, 22, 24–26, 37–38
Videos (library), 29
Volunteers file, 37

W

Weather gadget, 11–13
window(s)
    active, 16
    closing, 27
    displaying, 20–21
    hiding, 20–21
    maximizing, 19–20
    minimizing, 19–20
    moving, 24–27
    multiple open windows, 20, 22
    name, 15
    parts of, 5–6
    Personalization, 8–10
    resizing, 24–27
    restoring, 19–20
    scrolling, 24–27
    thumbnails of, 22
Windows 7, 3, 49
    Aero interface, 8, 21–23
    familiarization (Project 1A), 2–27
Windows Explorer, 5–6, 29–31
    defined, 5, 29
    navigating, 29–31
    opening, 29
    window, variances in, 5, 8
WinZip, 40
Word document files, 38
WordPad, 16

X-Y-Z

XML Files folder, 34, 40
zipped files, 40–42

SINGLE PC LICENSE AGREEMENT AND LIMITED WARRANTY

READ THIS LICENSE CAREFULLY BEFORE OPENING THIS PACKAGE. BY OPENING THIS PACKAGE, YOU ARE AGREEING TO THE TERMS AND CONDITIONS OF THIS LICENSE. IF YOU DO NOT AGREE, DO NOT OPEN THE PACKAGE. PROMPTLY RETURN THE UNOPENED PACKAGE AND ALL ACCOMPANYING ITEMS TO THE PLACE YOU OBTAINED THEM. *THESE TERMS APPLY TO ALL LICENSED SOFTWARE ON THE DISK EXCEPT THAT THE TERMS FOR USE OF ANY SHAREWARE OR FREEWARE ON THE DISKETTES ARE AS SET FORTH IN THE ELECTRONIC LICENSE LOCATED ON THE DISK:*

1. GRANT OF LICENSE and OWNERSHIP: The enclosed computer programs ("Software") are licensed, not sold, to you by Prentice-Hall, Inc. ("We" or the "Company") and in consideration of your purchase or adoption of the accompanying Company textbooks and/or other materials, and your agreement to these terms. We reserve any rights not granted to you. You own only the disk(s) but we and/or our licensors own the Software itself. This license allows you to use and display your copy of the Software on a single computer (i.e., with a single CPU) at a single location for academic use only, so long as you comply with the terms of this Agreement. You may make one copy for back up, or transfer your copy to another CPU, provided that the Software is usable on only one computer.

2. RESTRICTIONS: You may not transfer or distribute the Software or documentation to anyone else. Except for backup, you may not copy the documentation or the Software. You may not network the Software or otherwise use it on more than one computer or computer terminal at the same time. You may not reverse engineer, disassemble, decompile, modify, adapt, translate, or create derivative works based on the Software or the Documentation. You may be held legally responsible for any copying or copyright infringement which is caused by your failure to abide by the terms of these restrictions.

3. TERMINATION: This license is effective until terminated. This license will terminate automatically without notice from the Company if you fail to comply with any provisions or limitations of this license. Upon termination, you shall destroy the Documentation and all copies of the Software. All provisions of this Agreement as to limitation and disclaimer of warranties, limitation of liability, remedies or damages, and our ownership rights shall survive termination.

4. DISCLAIMER OF WARRANTY: THE COMPANY AND ITS LICENSORS MAKE NO WARRANTIES ABOUT THE SOFTWARE, WHICH IS PROVIDED "AS-IS." IF THE DISK IS DEFECTIVE IN MATERIALS OR WORKMANSHIP, YOUR ONLY REMEDY IS TO RETURN IT TO THE COMPANY WITHIN 30 DAYS FOR REPLACEMENT UNLESS THE COMPANY DETERMINES IN GOOD FAITH THAT THE DISK HAS BEEN MISUSED OR IMPROPERLY INSTALLED, REPAIRED, ALTERED OR DAMAGED. THE COMPANY DISCLAIMS ALL WARRANTIES, EXPRESS OR IMPLIED, INCLUDING WITHOUT LIMITATION, THE IMPLIED WARRANTIES OF MERCHANTABILITY AND FITNESS FOR A PARTICULAR PURPOSE. THE COMPANY DOES NOT WARRANT, GUARANTEE OR MAKE ANY REPRESENTATION REGARDING THE ACCURACY, RELIABILITY, CURRENTNESS, USE, OR RESULTS OF USE, OF THE SOFTWARE.

5. LIMITATION OF REMEDIES AND DAMAGES: IN NO EVENT, SHALL THE COMPANY OR ITS EMPLOYEES, AGENTS, LICENSORS OR CONTRACTORS BE LIABLE FOR ANY INCIDENTAL, INDIRECT, SPECIAL OR CONSEQUENTIAL DAMAGES ARISING OUT OF OR IN CONNECTION WITH THIS LICENSE OR THE SOFTWARE, INCLUDING, WITHOUT LIMITATION, LOSS OF USE, LOSS OF DATA, LOSS OF INCOME OR PROFIT, OR OTHER LOSSES SUSTAINED AS A RESULT OF INJURY TO ANY PERSON, OR LOSS OF OR DAMAGE TO PROPERTY, OR CLAIMS OF THIRD PARTIES, EVEN IF THE COMPANY OR AN AUTHORIZED REPRESENTATIVE OF THE COMPANY HAS BEEN ADVISED OF THE POSSIBILITY OF SUCH DAMAGES. SOME JURISDICTIONS DO NOT ALLOW THE LIMITATION OF DAMAGES IN CERTAIN CIRCUMSTANCES, SO THE ABOVE LIMITATIONS MAY NOT ALWAYS APPLY.

6. GENERAL: THIS AGREEMENT SHALL BE CONSTRUED IN ACCORDANCE WITH THE LAWS OF THE UNITED STATES OF AMERICA AND THE STATE OF NEW YORK, APPLICABLE TO CONTRACTS MADE IN NEW YORK, AND SHALL BENEFIT THE COMPANY, ITS AFFILIATES AND ASSIGNEES. This Agreement is the complete and exclusive statement of the agreement between you and the Company and supersedes all proposals, prior agreements, oral or written, and any other communications between you and the company or any of its representatives relating to the subject matter. If you are a U.S. Government user, this Software is licensed with "restricted rights" as set forth in subparagraphs (a)-(d) of the Commercial Computer-Restricted Rights clause at FAR 52.227-19 or in subparagraphs (c)(1)(ii) of the Rights in Technical Data and Computer Software clause at DFARS 252.227-7013, and similar clauses, as applicable.

Should you have any questions concerning this agreement or if you wish to contact the Company for any reason, please contact in writing:

Multimedia Production,
Higher Education Division,
Prentice-Hall, Inc.,
1 Lake Street,
Upper Saddle River NJ 07458.